WOMAN'S DAY
Prize-Winning Afghans

WOMAN'S DAY
Prize-Winning Afghans

THERESA CAPUANA, Needlework and Crafts Editor,
Woman's Day

SUSAN SIEGLER, Editor

Sedgewood® Press

NEW YORK

For Diamandis Communications Inc.

Editorial Director: *Geraldine Rhoads*
Needlework and Crafts Editor: *Theresa Capuana*
Project Editor: *Susan Siegler*
How-to Writer: *Ellen Liberles*
How-to Consultant: *Helen Donnally*
Illustrators: *Patrick O'Brien, Roberta Frauwirth*
Stylists: *Karen Lidbeck-Stewart, Holly-Dale Shapiro,*
    Woman's Day Needlework and Crafts Department
Administrative Assistant: *Grace Westing*
Photography: *William Seitz* 3, 7, 17, 22, 25, 37, 41, 45, 49,
    54, 58, 63, 68, 78, 94, 102, 111, 116, 120, 129, 140,
    147, 151, 155, 168, 173, 180
        Ben Calvo 98, 124, 143, 158, 164
        Julie Gang 29, 73, 83, 131

To the following, our special thanks for allowing us to photograph in their beautiful homes: Janice Parker, Joanne and Bill Seitz, Brenda and Nelson Slater, Susan and Jeffrey Weingarten.

For Sedgewood® Press

Director: *Elizabeth P. Rice*
Editorial Project Manager: *Susan Siegler*
Project Editor: *Gilda Abramowitz*
Production Manager: *Bill Rose*
Designer: *Antler & Baldwin Design Group*

Distributed by Macmillan Publishing Company, a division of Macmillan, Inc.

ISBN 0-02-496890-0
Library of Congress Catalog Card Number: 87-60953
Printed in the United States of America.

10 9 8 7 6 5 4 3 2 1

Introduction

Most of us don't have to check the dictionary to know that an afghan is a coverlet knitted or crocheted in strips or squares and tossed over the back of a sofa. But why is it named after a faraway country in Asia? Certainly no product of Afghanistan resembles this singularly American piece of needlework. What we do know is that our forebears were making them as far back as the 1830s. Perhaps to those early Victorians the geometric patterns of their work and the practice of draping it over furniture called to mind the rugs of the Middle East, and "afghan" became their voguish term for a decorative throw.

Whatever their reasoning, the Victorians had a good idea in the afghan. By the 1860s, Americans were turning them out with a vengeance. And they still are—for much the same purposes. A woolly lap robe to curl up in on a chilly evening is still just about as comforting as a mug of hot milk or a cuddly teddy bear. But a quick glance through this book will prove that afghans are more than just useful. They're works of art. These thirty-seven winners of the *Woman's Day* 1986 "Design-an-Afghan" contest are a museum-quality collection of unique and beautiful creations.

You might think that such exquisite works would be too difficult for all but the experienced needleworker. Not true. Afghans by their very size tend to be long-term projects. But many of these were designed with speed and simplicity in mind so they could be picked up and done whenever a busy woman could snatch a few minutes—often "while waiting for carpools, attending baseball games, watching TV, and on long car trips," as one woman put it.

Lots of these afghans, like Katherine Eng's "Fan Dance" (page 48), substitute a brilliant palette of colors for complicated stitchery. Other winners improvised shortcuts to make the job easy. Nancy Fuller, for example, found a way to eliminate the sewing together of all the little units of her "Garden Pathways" (page 62). Ruth Ramminger's use of a slip-stitch technique gave her "Reversible Rainbow" (page 115) a richness of pattern and texture that doesn't require an advanced degree in knitting. In fact, several entries were finished in a week. Margaret Hendrickson's painstaking design of "Whales Ahoy!" (page 77) took so much time that she had only two weeks to execute it, in simple single crochet and cross-stitch (it was a wedding gift for a couple of whale researchers). Dorothy Neidhart recalls that she didn't keep track of the time she put in on her "Paperweight Granny" (page 97) until, after watching about twenty hours of *Dallas*, *Knot's Landing*, and *Dynasty*, she realized she was halfway through.

That's not to imply that challenges don't abound among these afghans. Fran Weisse included in her "Marriage Lines" (page 179) seventeen different knitting-stitch patterns—each carefully chosen to symbolize something significant in the lives of her brother and new sister-in-law. Every one of the twenty-nine stripes in Linda Stephens's "Striped Odyssey" (page 146) is a different crochet pattern.

But, easy or difficult, what makes the afghans in this collection so valuable is the artistry of the designs. Practically every one comes from an avid knitter or crocheter who, like Judith Braithwaite, has a history of "sweaters, booties, bonnets, baby afghans, doilies, lace edging, a round tablecloth, and fifteen full-size afghans." They inundate family members with gifts of their handiwork. They have huge sacks of scrap yarn waiting to be used on new projects. Their flying needles and hooks are the mainstay of local fund-raising bazaars and craft fairs. They are regular prize winners at the county fair. For these women, an afghan is their artist's canvas. With yarn and stitches, they paint their particular creative vision.

Their inspiration can be as simple as the Christmas potholder that Jean Cates recolored and expanded into her "Flower Petals and Lace" (page 36). It might come from the vivid tartan plaids that were re-created in crochet by Marion Currie (page 44) and Faye Sharpe (page 139). But many take their designs from the world around them. The great sweep of North America is represented here—from the streets of New Bedford (Judith Gurney's "New Bedford, Massachusetts, 50 Years Ago," page 72) to the vineyards of California (Jewel Gotelli's "Grape Trellis," page 67) to the mountains of British Columbia (June Forrester's "Canadian Evergreens," page 57). Jeanne Crooks (page 40) and Felicia Nelson (page 101) drew on American Indian motifs. And a whole group of winners translated typical American quilt patterns into much-quicker-to-finish crochet or knit designs. You'll find an Amish Fan (page 48), a Cat's Paw (page 154), and a Texas Star (page 163) pattern among other clever takeoffs.

Most pervasive of all is that granddaddy of afghan patterns, the granny square. Marsha Horstmann turned hers into tiny bear faces with stuffed noses (page 82). Marion Tuthill translated hers into a quilt design (page 163). Joan Stagg embellished hers with popcorns (page 142). Sandra Oidtman made hers into baby blocks (page 110). There are also several traditional granny-square renditions, almost mesmerizing in the beauty of their brilliant combinations of jewellike colors or soft pastels.

What comes through in so many of these works is the scope an afghan gives its designer to express an idea or sentiment or to preserve a memory. For example, Linda McGregor Scott's "Child's World" (page 130) was inspired by a patchwork quilt of her grandmother's. "As a child, I spent hours 'driving' toy cars over the designs, which in my imagination became houses and roads. I wanted my son, Aaron, to experience the same joy." So she crisscrossed her afghan with "places and times important in a child's world, such as church, school, the zoo, fire department, police station, a grocery store, the seashore, Easter, Halloween, and the palm-treed home where he once lived in Florida." The work, she tells us, never became monotonous, because the blocks of designs were as unlimited as her imagination.

Some people welcome the monotony of working repeat patterns in an afghan. One thing we've noticed in putting together this winning collection: afghan makers seem to fall into two distinctly different camps. There are those who enjoy keeping their hands busy but their minds unengaged, so that, as Kathryn Rogers says, "I can do it while my eyes are doing something else." Others insist on a design that's intricate enough, as Kathy Carr says, "to hold my attention to the pattern." Whether you like the soothing rhythm of creating something beautiful while you watch TV or want to be totally absorbed every stitch of the way, we're sure you'll find just the right design in this book to give you many hours of pleasure. Perhaps you'll even be stimulated to develop your own design—one that uniquely expresses your view of life.

Contents

This listing indicates the needlework technique used for each design, whether the work is portable, and which projects seem best suited to the beginner, to the experienced needleworker, or to the in-betweener with some experience.

However, do read the instructions for any afghan that captures your fancy, and decide for yourself whether it offers a challenge you'll enjoy.

More than half of the afghans are made in several—or many—pieces, and in many instances the individual units are relatively easy to work. But in reaching their judgments the editors considered the complexity and length of instructions or how complicated the final assembly might seem, as well as the facility needed to execute the basic design.

THE AFGHANS

GENERAL DIRECTIONS

Millefleur

A good portable project, a spread crocheted in 99
pieces by Mary Beth Alexander of Columbia, Tennessee

Scattered flowers against a midnight-black background
create a dramatic Victorian effect.

About Mary Beth Alexander

"Afghans had never really interested me until I ran out
of room for all the sweaters I was making," Mary Beth
Alexander says. As for "Millefleur," she began it before
she met her husband, in an attempt to earn some
money with her hobby. She chose the colors from
scraps she had on hand, "the motifs were easy to carry
to work, and I had spare time there to work on it." By
the time "Millefleur" was completed, after her
marriage, the afghan had so many admirers she
couldn't bear to sell it. Mary Beth continues to be an
avid crocheter: "In the evening while the TV is on I
feel lost without hook and yarn in my hands."

SIZE: About 63″ × 77″

MATERIALS: Yarn: Knitting worsted, 12 oz black, plus an additional 65 oz scraps in assorted solid and variegated colors (use either all wool or all synthetic yarn throughout); **crochet hook:** size H (5.00 mm) *or size that gives you the correct gauge.*

GAUGE: Each motif measures about 7″ across from point to point.

FLOWER MOTIF: Make 99. Each motif is worked in any 2 colors; black is used for joining and for Square Motifs only. Starting at center with first color, ch 4. **Rnd 1:** Work 7 dc in 4th ch from hook. Mark beg of rnds. Do not join, but work around and around. **Rnd 2:** Work 2 sc in top of ch 3, * sc in next dc, 2 sc in next dc; repeat from * around, ending with sc in last dc (12 sc). **Rnd 3:** * Work 2 sc in next sc, sc in next 2 sc; repeat from * around, ending sc in last 2 sc (16 sc). **Rnd 4:** Sc in next sc, * ch 7, sc in 2nd ch from hook and in each remaining ch of ch 7 (a petal made), sc in next 2 sc of previous rnd; repeat from * around, ending with sc in last sc (8 petals). **Rnd 5:** * Working in unworked side of next petal, sc in next 6 ch, 3 sc in ch at tip, sc in each of next 6 sc on other edge of petal, skip 2 sc between petals; repeat from * around, ending by working around last petal. Break off first color; attach 2nd color. **Rnd 6:** * Skip first sc on next petal, sc in next 6 sc, work 3 sc in next sc (tip of petal), sc in next 6 sc, skip last sc on petal; repeat from * around. Repeat Rnd 6 twice more. Sl st in next sc. Break off. *Note:* Motif edge may be rippled.

Work motifs, varying color combinations.

ASSEMBLY: Lay out Flower Motifs in desired color arrangement, having 11 rows of 9 motifs each. Scatter colors as evenly as possible throughout. Make sure that similarly colored motifs are not next to each other or placed so that all-dark or all-bright motifs are concentrated in one area.

Joining: See Joining Diagram. Join motifs as follows: attach black to petal tip (point a) of a corner motif (motif 1), sc in next 6 sc of petal, skip next 2 sc (last sc of petal and first sc of next petal); continue to work around edge in this manner, around points b and c, ending at d and skipping 2 sc between petals; attach motif 2 by working

Joining Diagram

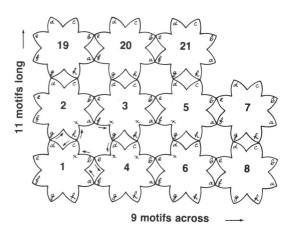

11 motifs long

9 motifs across

4

sc at tip of petal (point g on motif 2); working as before, sc around edge of motif 2 to point h; now work sc back into motif 1 at point c; sc along edge of motif 2 around to point a; attach motif 3 by working sc at tip of petal (point f on motif 3); sc around edge of motif 3 to point g; attach motif 4 by working sc at tip of petal (point d on motif 4); sc around edge of motif 4 to point e; attach to motif 1 by working sc back into motif 1 at point b, then sc along edge of motif 4 around to point f, sc into motif 1 at point a. Break off.

Square Motif: With black, ch 3. **Rnd 1:** Work 4 sc in 3rd ch from hook. Mark beg of rnds. Work around and around. **Rnd 2:** Work 2 sc in each sc (8 sc). **Rnd 3:** * Sc in next sc, in next sc work (sc, ch 1, sc) for corner; repeat from * 3 times more. **Rnd 4:** Sc in each sc to first corner ch-1 sp, * in corner sp work corner of (sc, ch 1, sc), sc to next corner sp; repeat from * twice more, work corner in sp, sc in last sc. **Rnd 5** (joining rnd): (*Note:* In order to simplify the Joining Diagram, the Square Motifs have been omitted.) Sc in each sc to first corner sp, in sp work sc, then sc into motif 1 at x (between petals), sc in same sp of Square Motif; sc to next corner sp, sc in sp, sc into x of motif 4, sc into same sp of Square Motif; continue around, joining corners to x of 3rd motif, then 2nd motif, sc to end; sl st to first sc of rnd. Break off.

To join next 2 motifs, attach black to point a of motif 4, sc around points a, b, and c, ending at d, sc into motif 3 at g, sc along motif 3 to h, sc back into motif 4 at c, sc along motif 3 to a, sc into motif 5 at f, sc along motif 5 to g, sc into motif 6 at d, sc along motif 6 to e, sc back into motif 4 at b, sc along motif 6 to f, sc back into motif 4 at a. Break off. Work Square Motif as before, attaching corners to x of motifs 4, 6, 5, and 3.

Attach black to point a of motif 6 and join next 2 motifs in same manner as before. Work Square Motif in space between 4 motifs. Continue in this manner, joining 2 motifs, until a strip of 2 rows of 9 motifs each is formed, with 8 Square Motifs worked in spaces.

Attach black to a of motif 2 and join motifs 19 and 20 in same manner. Work Square Motif in space. Attach black to a of motif 3 and join motif 21 in same manner. Continue to work across row, joining new motifs and working a Square Motif in each space. Continue to add rows until there are 11 rows of 9 motifs each.

Flower Fantasia

A third-prize winner, in afghan stitch and cross-stitch embroidery, by Johnnie Angell of Beaverton, Oregon

Leftover yarn scraps in vivid colors echo the bright flowers in the designer's garden.

About Johnnie Angell

Johnnie Angell's afghan displays the flowers that bloom on the one-acre suburban homesite she and her husband share with "an assortment of dogs, cats, birds, and one horse." The horse, "a pretty Morgan mare," Johnnie says, "has owned *us* for twelve years." A prolific knitter and crocheter, Johnnie found herself with sacks of leftover yarn, most of it in off-white. "The off-white was logical for a background, but since the dye lots didn't match exactly, I decided to make squares or rectangles out of it," with the amount of yarn often deciding the size of a square. When she pieced her thirty-four panels together, she just added extra borders where needed to fit her flower puzzle together.

SIZE: About 63″ × 75″

MATERIALS: Yarn: Knitting worsted, about 7 lb (112 oz) natural white (MC), about 2 oz each assorted colors (see color key with charts); **afghan hook:** size I (5.50 mm) *or the size that gives you the correct gauge;* **crochet hook:** size I; tapestry needle.

GAUGE: With afghan hook, 4 sts = 1″; 4 rows = 1″.

Note: This afghan is made of 34 blocks of various sizes that are worked in plain afghan stitch, then embroidered and sewn together, with a crocheted border added.

PATTERN STITCH: Plain Afghan Stitch. See Plain Afghan Stitch, page 195.

BLOCKS: Starting at lower edge of block with afghan hook and MC, ch number of sts specified (see below) plus 1 st more. For Block 1, for instance, ch 32 to work 31 sts. Work each block the specified number of rows, then sl st in each st across last row. Fasten off. As you complete each block, pin to it a slip of paper with its number, so you can correctly identify blocks later for assembly and embroidery.

Block 1 (mountain asters): 31 sts × 44 rows. **Block 2 (fuchsia):** 35 sts × 21 rows. **Block 3 (violets):** 22 sts × 22 rows. **Block 4 (California poppies):** 72 sts × 42 rows. **Block 5 (water iris):** 62 sts × 55 rows. **Block 6 (goldenrod, cattails, and daisies):** 31 sts × 61 rows. **Block 7 (roses):** 62 sts × 56 rows. **Block 8 (impatiens):** 47 sts × 34 rows. **Block 9 (morning glory):** 17 sts × 34 rows. **Block 10 (wild roses):** 42 sts × 20 rows. **Block 11 (pansy):** 22 sts × 21 rows. **Block 12 (violets):** 117 sts × 20 rows. **Block 13 (daffodils):** 63 sts × 56 rows. **Block 14 (tulips):** 22 sts × 78 rows. **Block 15 (zinnias):** 55 sts × 24 rows. **Block 16 (water lily):** 25 sts × 16 rows. **Block 17 (clover):** 22 sts × 16 rows. **Block 18 (delphiniums):** 62 sts × 56 rows. **Block 19 (poppy):** 26 sts × 56 rows. **Block 20 (primroses);** 62 sts × 20 rows. **Block 21 (rose):** 47 sts × 39 rows. **Block 22 (cyclamens):** 48 sts × 24 rows. **Block 23 (crocus):** 22 sts × 24 rows. **Block 24 (nasturtiums):** 62 sts × 56 rows. **Block 25 (pansies):** 20 sts × 20 rows. **Block 26 (marigolds):** 21 sts × 24 rows. **Block 27 (lilacs):** 62 sts × 56 rows. **Block 28 (calla lilies):** 31 sts × 56 rows. **Block 29 (clematis):** 21 sts × 25 rows. **Block 30 (orchid):** 22 sts × 24 rows. **Block 31 (poinsettias):** 52 sts × 30 rows. **Block 32 (forget-me-nots):** 50 sts × 27 rows. **Block 33 (thistles):** 25 sts × 27 rows. **Block 34 (bachelor's buttons):** 32 sts × 27 rows.

BLOCK BORDERS: When all blocks are completed, arrange them on a flat surface in order shown in Layout Chart, lining up outer edges of edge blocks in a straight line and leaving about 2″ space between blocks. *Note:* The space between blocks varies slightly, with some spaces less than 2″ and some more. To join blocks smoothly, work as the designer did, adjusting the width of border on each block edge as needed to fit perfectly (see below for how to adjust width).

Basic Block Border (about 1″ wide): Crochet around each block as follows. **Rnd 1:** With right side of work facing you, using crochet hook and MC, sc evenly around block, working 3 sc at each corner; join. **Rnd 2:** Ch 3 (counts as 1 dc); working in back loop only of each st, dc in each sc around, working 3 dc in center st at each corner; join. Fasten off. *For wider border,* add another row of sc, or dc as needed. *For narrower border,* omit 2nd row or work 2nd row in sc. Block pieces so edges match up exactly.

EMBROIDERY: See Cross-Stitch over Afghan Stitch, page 195. When blocks are completed, work cross-stitch embroidery on each, following charts and color key.

ASSEMBLY: Again arrange blocks on a flat surface in order shown in Layout Chart. Butt edges and sew together with MC, either overcasting or weaving.

AFGHAN BORDER: (*Note:* Work in back loop only of each st throughout.) **Rnd 1:** With right side facing you, using crochet hook and MC, work sc evenly spaced around afghan, working 3 sc in center st at each corner; join. **Rnd 2:** * Skip next st, work (sc, hdc, dc) in next st, tr in next st, work (dc, hdc, sc) in next st, skip next st, sl st in next st (scallop made); repeat from * around, omitting skipped sts when making scallop at each corner and adjusting number of sts skipped along sides, if necessary, so repeat works out evenly along each side; join. **Rnd 3:** * Sl st in next sc, (ch 3, sc in next st) 5 times, sl st in next sc, sl st in sl st; repeat from * around; join. Fasten off.

Color Key

▲ = dk brown
✗ = med brown
+ = tan
• = pale yellow
� = canary yellow
T = tangerine
● = dk red
V = bright red
S = hot pink
⊠ = deep rose
P = dk rose
∴ = pink
I = pale pink
X = dk green
╱ = med green
⅂ = lt green
◣ = deep violet
G = purple
◊ = lt purple
L = lavender
◖ = dk blue
O = med blue
— = lt blue
■ = black

9

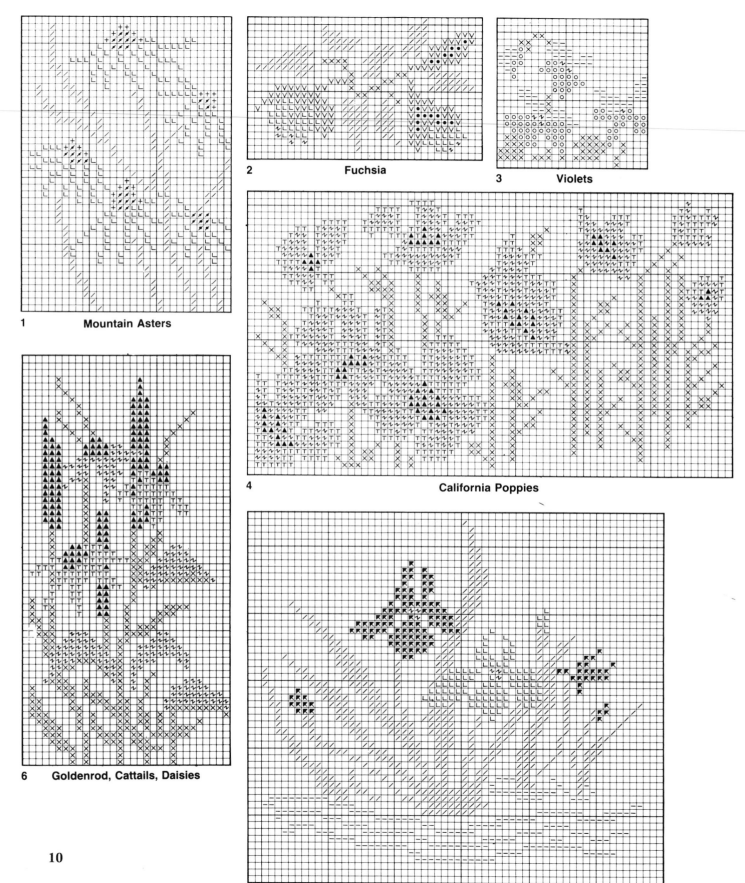

1   Mountain Asters

2   Fuchsia

3   Violets

4   California Poppies

6   Goldenrod, Cattails, Daisies

5   Water Iris

10

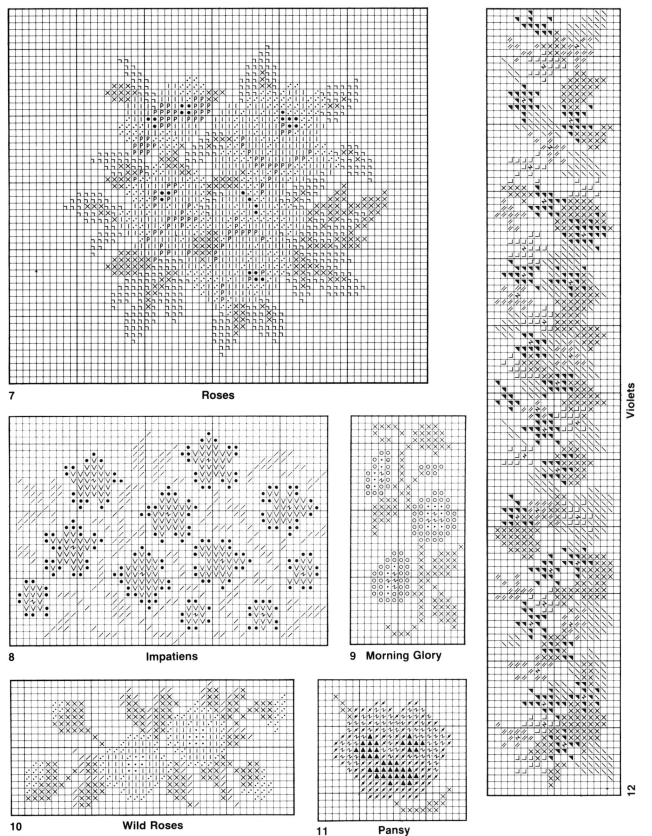

7   **Roses**

8   **Impatiens**

9   **Morning Glory**

10   **Wild Roses**

11   **Pansy**

Violets

12

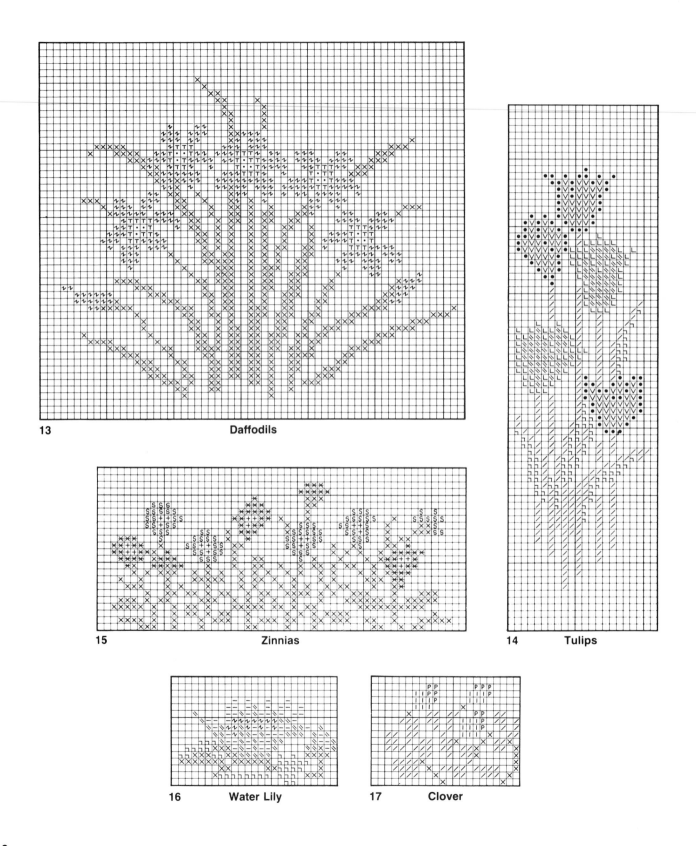

13   **Daffodils**

15   **Zinnias**

14   **Tulips**

16   **Water Lily**

17   **Clover**

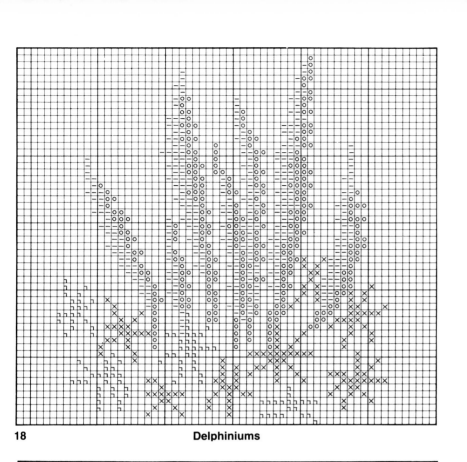

18 **Delphiniums**

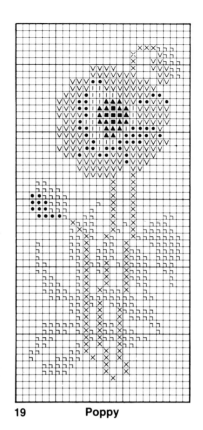

19 **Poppy**

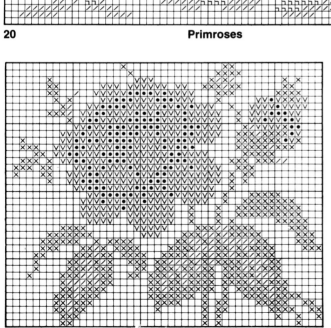

20 **Primroses**

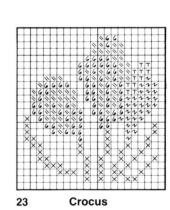

23 **Crocus**

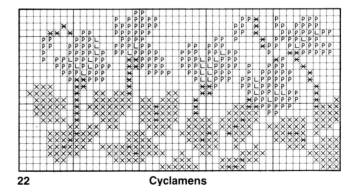

22 **Cyclamens**

21 **Rose**

13

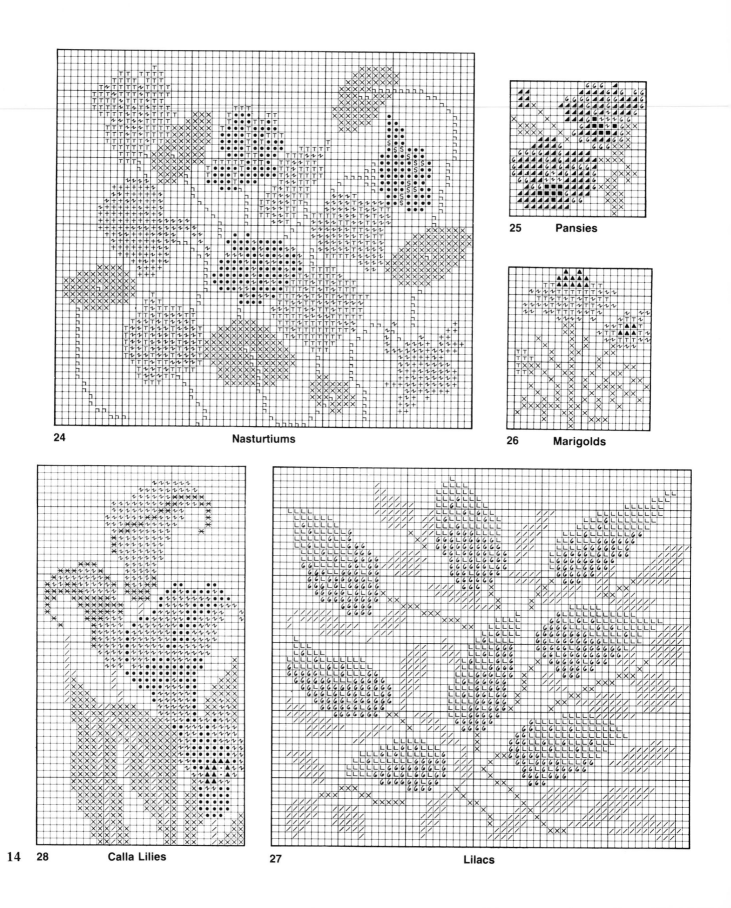

24   **Nasturtiums**

25   **Pansies**

26   **Marigolds**

14   **28**   **Calla Lilies**

27   **Lilacs**

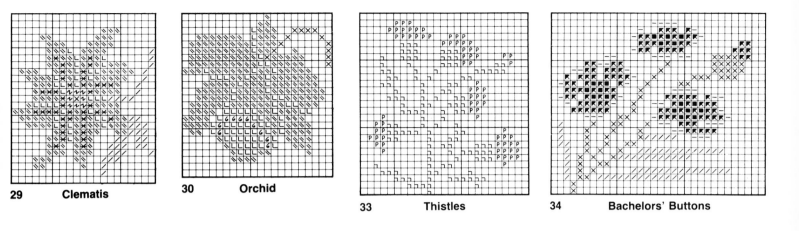

29 Clematis

30 Orchid

33 Thistles

34 Bachelors' Buttons

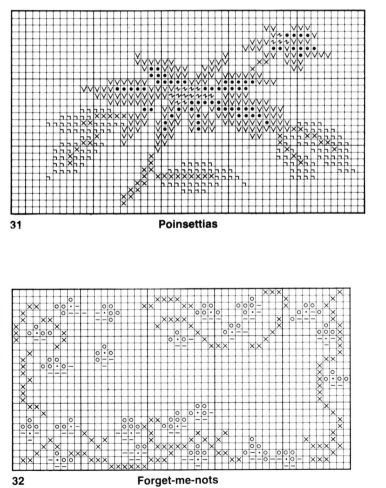

31 Poinsettias

32 Forget-me-nots

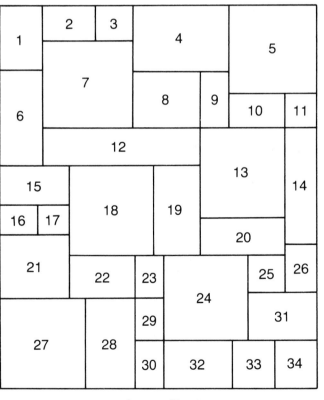

Layout Chart

15

Oriental Medallion

The grand-prize-winning afghan, crocheted and cross-stitched by Renatè Brigitte Austin of Montpelier, Vermont

Single crochet embellished with counted cross-stitch produces this stunning tour de force, a replica of an Oriental medallion carpet.

About Renatè Brigitte Austin

Renatè Austin learned the basics of needlework around age six from her mother in Germany. She says she participates in many crafts shows, but this is the first needlework she ever entered in a contest, and she plans to keep the afghan as a family treasure to be passed on. Highly skilled in her craft, Renatè tells us it took her one week to complete this piece. "I worked on it whenever I had a chance—sometimes only one or two rows at a time. The basic single crochet is easy and the material works up fast. The fun part is the embroidery." She took her design from Oriental rugs, to provide an accent for the light and simple furniture in her Vermont living room. It can also complement Victorian decor, as we show it.

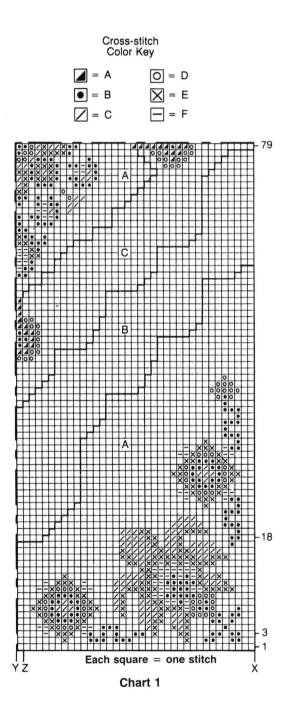

Cross-stitch Color Key

◪ = A ⊙ = D
⊙ = B ⊠ = E
◪ = C ⊟ = F

Each square = one stitch

Chart 1

SIZE: About 52″ × 67″

MATERIALS: Yarn: Knitting worsted, 32 oz rust (color A), 21 oz dark blue (B), 14 oz white (C), 7 oz light blue (D), 4 oz each rose (E) and gold (F); **crochet hook:** size G (4.50 mm) *or the size that gives you the correct gauge;* tapestry needle.

GAUGE: 7 sc = 2″; 4 rows = 1″.

Note: Afghan is worked in crocheted panels that are embroidered in cross-stitch.

CENTER PANEL: *Note:* To change colors in sc, work off last 2 loops of last sc of old color with next color. Do not carry colors across row; use a separate ball of yarn for each section.

Starting at one end of panel with A, ch 74. **Row 1:** Sc in 2nd ch from hook and in each remaining ch across (73 sc). Ch 1, turn. **Row 2 (right side):** Sc in each sc across. Ch 1, turn. Repeating Row 2 for pattern st, work for 15 more rows. Follow Chart 1, beginning with Row 18, for large outlined areas A, B, C, and A; do not follow symbols, which are for cross-stitches to be worked later. *To follow chart,* read each row from X to Y, then from Z back to X; work Rows 18 through 79 (center row), then 78 back to 1. Fasten off.

Embroidery: Following symbols on Chart 1, embroider design in cross-stitch (see stitch instructions on page 195), working each stitch over 1 sc.

Center Panel Border: All rnds are worked from right side. **Rnd 1:** With B, * sc in end of each row across one long edge of center panel (157 sc), ch 2 for corner, sc in each st across end of panel (73 sc), ch 2 for corner; repeat from * once more; join with sl st to first sc. **Rnd 2:** Ch 4, * skip 1 sc, dc in next sc, ch 1; repeat from * to next corner, work (dc, ch 1) 3 times in corner sp, dc in first sc on next side, ch 1; repeat from * around, ending with (dc, ch 1) 3 times at last corner; join to 3rd ch of ch 4. **Rnd 3:** Sc in same place as joining, sc in each ch-1 sp and each dc around, working 3 dc in center dc at each corner; join. Fasten off. **Rnd 4:** With A, sc in each sc, working 3 sc in center st at corners. Fasten off. **Rnd 5:** Join C in first st after corner st at beg of long edge; repeat Rnd 4. **Rnd 6:** Using C and D, enclosing 2nd color in sts when not in use, with C sc in first 3 sc, completing last sc with D; *

with D work popcorn as follows: work 5 sc in next sc, remove hook and insert it from front in first D sc and through dropped loop, with C yo and draw through all loops on hook, ch 1 (popcorn made); with C sc in next 7 sc, completing last sc with D; repeat from *, ending as established in st before next corner st, work 3 sc in corner st; working across end, sc in first 6 sc, repeat from *, ending as established at corner, work 3 sc in corner st, 4 sc on next long edge; repeat from * around; join. **Rnd 7:** With C, sc around, working popcorn with D in sts before and after each popcorn on previous rnd, working sc with C in top of each popcorn, and working 3 sc at corners; join. *Note:* From now on, work 3 sc at each corner unless otherwise noted. **Rnd 8:** With C, sc around, working popcorn with D over center sc between each pair of popcorns. Cut D. **Rnd 9:** With C, sc in each sc and in each popcorn around; join. Fasten off. **Rnd 10:** With A, sc in each sc around; join. Fasten off.

SIDE PANELS: Row 1: From right side, attach A to corner st at beginning of one long side of center panel border; sc in same sc and in each sc across, ending at corner st. Ch 1, turn. **Rows 2 through 16:** Sc in each sc. Ch 1, turn. Fasten off. Work panel on opposite long edge.

    Embroidery: Following Chart 2 and matching center st to center of panel, embroider cross-stitch designs on side panels.

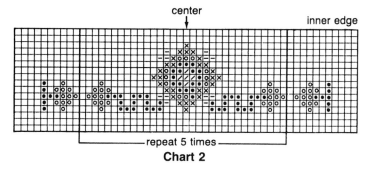

Chart 2

MESH BORDER: Rnd 1: From right side, attach B to first st after corner at beginning of long edge, sc in each st around, working 3 sc in corners; join. **Rnd 2:** Ch 4, * skip next sc, dc in next sc, ch 1; repeat from * to next corner st, work (dc, ch 1) 3 times in corner st; repeat from * around; join to 3rd ch of ch 4. **Rnd 3:** Sc in each ch and each dc, working 3 sc in center dc at corners; join. Fasten off. **Rnd 4:** With A, repeat Rnd 3.

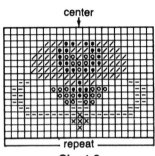

center
↑

repeat

Chart 3

END PANELS: Row 1: With right side or work facing you, beginning in corner st with A, sc in each sc across end of afghan to next corner st; ch 1, turn. Work 16 more rows of sc. Fasten off. Repeat on other end of afghan.

OUTER SIDE PANELS: Row 1: With right side of work facing you, with A, sc in end of each row and in each sc on a long edge. Work 16 more rows of sc. Fasten off. Repeat on other long edge.

    Embroidery: Following Chart 3, begin in center of each panel and embroider design 5 times across end panels and 9 times across outer side panels, adjusting spacing if necessary.

OUTER BORDERS: Rnds 1, 2, and 3: With B, repeat Rnds 1, 2, and 3 of Mesh Border. Fasten off. Beginning in first st on a long side, with C, work 2 rnds sc. **Rnd 6:** With D, work popcorn in first sc, * with C sc in next 3 sc, with D work popcorn in next sc; repeat from * around, working 3 sc at corners, 2 more before first popcorn on long edges, and 1 before first popcorn on ends. **Rnds 7 and 8:** With C, sc around. **Rnds 9 through 13:** With B, work Mesh Border Rnds 1, 2, 3, 2, 3. Fasten off.

EDGINGS: Row 1: With right side facing you, working across end of afghan, attach B to corner st; sc in corner st, ch 4, * skip 3 sc, work (dc, ch 1) 3 times in next sc (shell made); skip 3 sc, ch 1, dc in next sc, ch 1; repeat from * across, ending dc in corner and adjusting skipped sts as necessary. Ch 1, turn. **Row 2:** Sc in first dc, sc in next ch-1 space, * 2 sc in ch-1 space of shell, ch 3, sc in first ch of ch 3 (picot made over center dc of shell), 2 sc in next ch-1 sp, 1 sc in each of next 2 ch-1 sp; repeat from *, ending sc in 3rd ch of ch 4. Fasten off. Work edging on opposite end.

Reversible Tiles

Double-knit throw by Marion Boright of
Manchester Center, Vermont

Double knitting produces a two-layered stockinette-
stitch fabric, with the smooth knit surface facing out on
both sides. The afghan is reversible and extra warm.

About Marion Boright

The design for Marion Boright's afghan was conceived
years before she thought of using it for a stitchery
project. Originally she charted it as a tile pattern to
adorn a gas fireplace. When a move canceled her
decorating plans, she filed it away for future use. It
was a double-knit sweater from Mexico that inspired
her to try double knitting an afghan. "I am a
moderately experienced knitter," she says, "and it
didn't look that hard." As she started to teach herself,
however, "my first efforts were laughable. Then I saw
that it really boiled down to a simple 'knit one, purl
one' ribbing, only with two colors. Soon I was doing it
as easily as ribbing."

SIZE: About 45″ × 49″, plus 3″ fringes

MATERIALS: Yarn: Knitting worsted, 24 oz each light peach (color A) and dark coral (B); **knitting needles:** 36″-long circular needle size 10 (6.00 mm) *or the size that gives you the correct gauge;* **crochet hook:** size I (5.50 mm).

GAUGE: 3 (k 1, p 1) units = 1″; 9 rows = 2″.

Note: Afghan is worked in one piece in double knitting. See Double Knit, page 201, and make a practice swatch before beginning afghan. **Units:** *A unit* means k 1 A, yf, p 1 B, yb. *B unit* means k 1 B, yf, p 1 A, yb.

AFGHAN: Starting at one end, with A and B, cast on 266 sts, alternating colors. Do not join sts on circular needle, but work back and forth in rows. **Row 1:** Work A units (see Note above) across row. **Row 2:** Work B units across. Repeat these 2 rows 3 times, ending with Row 8 on chart. **Row 9:** Work 5 units A, (59 units B, 5 units A) twice. **Row 10:** Work 5 units B, (59 units A, 5 units B) twice. Continue following chart from 11th row, reading chart from X to Z once, then Y to Z once. (*Note:* Design appears elongated on chart; knitted design, however, will be almost square.) Following color key carefully to work reversible design, complete chart, then work from Row 8 to Row 112 once more to complete 4 tile motifs. Bind off.

FINISHING: Border: Rnd 1: With A, crochet row of sc around afghan, spacing sts to keep edges smooth and flat and working 3 sc at each corner. **Rnd 2:** Sc in each sc around, working 3 sc in center sc at each corner.

FRINGE: See Fringes, page 196. For each fringe cut one strand of B, 6½″ long. Make fringe in each sc across both narrow ends of afghan.

Reverse Side

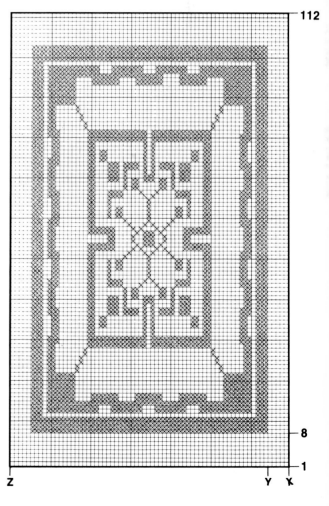

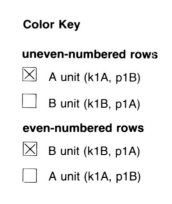

Color Key

uneven-numbered rows

☒   A unit (k1A, p1B)

☐   B unit (k1B, p1A)

even-numbered rows

☒   B unit (k1B, p1A)

☐   A unit (k1A, p1B)

23

Irish Lace

Knitted bedspread combining four popular sweater patterns, by Judith Braithwaite of Orem, Utah

This Aran-style classic employs enough openwork to make it a lovely, light coverlet.

About Judith Braithwaite

Judith Braithwaite's father taught her to knit when she was a girl. "He learned during World War I, when schoolchildren knitted gloves and sock tops for the soldiers," says Judith. The mother of ten children, and grandmother of four, Judith started her knitting "career" by making dishcloths from rug yarn. Since those early efforts, she has created "sweaters, booties, bonnets, baby afghans, doilies, lace edging, a round tablecloth, and fifteen full-size afghans." This handsome afghan was made extra-long to accommodate a son who is 6'5".

SIZE: About 80″ × 80″, plus 7″ fringe

MATERIALS: Yarn: Knitting worsted, 92 oz natural white (see note under Fringe, below); **knitting needles:** 36″-long circular needle size 10½ (6.50 mm) *or the size that gives you the correct gauge.*

GAUGE: In pattern, average 4 sts = 1″; 5 rows = 1″.

PATTERN A: Worked on 22 sts. **Row 1 and all wrong-side rows:** P 10, k 2, p 10. **Row 2 (right side):** K 6, then work right dec-2 (Rdec-2) as follows: sl 1, k 1, psso, sl first st on right-hand needle back to left-hand needle, k 2 tog (Rdec-2 made); yo, k 1, yo, p 2, yo, k 1, yo, make left dec-2 (Ldec-2) as follows: sl 1, k 2 tog, psso (Ldec-2 made), k 6. **Row 4:** K 4, work Rdec-2, (k 1, yo) twice, k 1, p 2, (k 1, yo) twice, k 1, work Ldec-2, k 4. **Row 6:** K 2, Rdec-2, k 2, yo, k 1, yo, k 2, p 2, k 2, yo, k 1, yo, k 2, Ldec-2, 2. **Row 8:** Rdec-2, k 3, yo, k 1, yo, k 3, p 2, k 3, yo, k 1, yo, k 3, Ldec-2. Repeat Rows 1 through 8 for pattern.

PATTERN B: Worked on 14 sts. **Row 1 and all wrong-side rows:** (K 1, yarn forward, sl 1, yarn back) 3 times, k 3, p 5. **Row 2 (right side):** Yo, sl 1, k 1, psso, k 3, yo, work bobble on 2 sts as follows: into next st work k in front loop, then back loop, front loop, back loop (4 loops in 1 st), k next st and pass 4 loops, one by one, over this k st (bobble made), p 1, (k 1, p 1) 3 times. **Row 4:** K 1, yo, sl 1, k 1, psso, k 2, p 3, (k 1, p 1) 3 times. **Row 6:** K 2, yo, sl 1, k 1, psso, k 1, p 3, (k 1, p 1) 3 times. **Row 8:** K 3, yo, sl 1, k 1, psso, p 3, (k 1, p 1) 3 times. Repeat Rows 1 through 8 for pattern.

PATTERN C: Worked on 21 sts. **Row 1:** K 9, p 3, k 9. **Row 2 (right side):** P 9, k 3, p 9. **Row 3:** Repeat Row 1. **Row 4:** P 8, k 2 tog, yo, k 1, yo, sl 1, k 1, psso, p 8. **Row 5:** K 8, p 5, k 8. **Row 6:** P 7, k 2 tog, k 1, (yo, k 1) twice, sl 1, k 1, psso, p 7. **Row 7:** K 7, p 7, k 7. **Row 8:** P 6, k 2 tog, k 2, yo, k 1, yo, k 2, sl 1, k 1, psso, p 6. **Row 9:** K 6, p 9, k 6. **Row 10:** P 5, k 2 tog, k 3, yo, k 1, yo, k 3, sl 1, k 1, psso, p 5. **Row 11:** K 5, p 11, k 5. **Row 12:** P 4, k 2 tog, k 4, yo, k 1, yo, k 4, sl 1, k 1, psso, p 4. **Row 13:** K 4, p 13, k 4. **Row 14:** P 4, sl 1, k 1, psso, k 4, yo, k 1, yo, k 4, k 2 tog, p 4. **Row 15:** Repeat Row 13. **Row 16:** P 4, sl 1, k 1, psso, k 3, (yo, k 3) twice, k 2 tog, p 4. **Row 17:** Repeat Row 13. **Row 18:** P 4, sl 1, k 1, psso, k 2, yo, k 2 tog, yo, k 1, yo, sl 1, k 1, psso, yo, k 2, k 2 tog, p 4. **Row 19:** Repeat Row 13. **Row 20:** P 4, sl 1, k 1, psso, k 1, yo, k 2 tog, yo, k 3, yo, sl 1, k 1, psso, yo, k 1, k 2 tog, p 4. **Row 21:** Repeat Row 13. **Row 22:** P 4, sl 1, k 1, psso, k 1, yo, sl 1, k 1, psso, yo, k 3, yo, k 2 tog, yo, k 1, k 2 tog, p 4. **Row 23:** Repeat Row 9. **Row 24:** P 7, yo, sl 1, k 1, psso, yo, sl 1, k 2 tog, psso, yo, k 2 tog, yo, p 7. **Row 25:** Repeat Row 7. **Row 26:** P 8, yo, sl 1, k 1, psso, k 1, k 2 tog, yo, p 8. **Row 27:** Repeat Row 5. **Row 28:** P 9, yo, sl 1, k 2 tog, psso, yo, p 9. **Row 29:** Repeat Row 1. **Row 30:** P 21. **Row 31:** K 21. **Row 32:** P 21. Repeat Rows 1 through 32 for pattern.

PATTERN D: Worked on 14 sts. **Row 1 and all wrong-side rows:** P 5, k 3, (yarn forward, sl 1, yarn back, k 1) 3 times. **Row 2 (right side):** (P 1, k 1) 3 times, p 1, work bobble on 2 sts same as for Row 2 of Pattern B, yo, k 3, k 2 tog, yo. **Row 4:** (P 1, k 1) 3 times, p 3, k 2, k 2 tog, yo, k 1. **Row 6:** (P 1, k 1) 3 times, p 3, k 1, k 2 tog, yo, k 2. **Row 8:** (P 1, k 1) 3 times, p 3, k 2 tog, yo, k 3. Repeat Rows 1 through 8 for pattern.

AFGHAN: Cast on 316 sts. Do not join, but work back and forth on circular needle and k 8 rows for garter-st border. **Next row (wrong side):** K 5 (garter–st border), place marker on needle, work Row 1 of Pattern A on next 22 sts, place another marker on needle, * work Row 1 of Pattern B on next 14 sts, marker, Pattern C on next 21 sts, marker, Pattern D on next 14 sts, marker, Pattern A on next 22 sts, marker; repeat from * 3 times more, k last 5 sts for garter-st border. **Next row (right side):** K 5 (border), slip marker, work Row 2 of Pattern A, slip marker, * work Row 2 of Patterns D, C, B, and A; repeat from * 3 times more, k 5 (border). Keeping 5 sts at beg and end of row in garter st and slipping the markers between patterns in each row, continue in patterns as established until Pattern C has been worked 12 times in length. K 8 rows for garter-st border. Bind off.

FRINGE: *Note:* On original afghan, fringe was added only to cast-on edge of afghan. If you wish to add fringe to bound-off edge as well, purchase extra yarn. See Fringes, page 196. For each fringe cut eight 15″ strands. Make fringe every 1″ along edge of afghan.

Circus Time!

Child's bedspread (or hanging) knitted by Kathy Carr
of Erie, Pennsylvania

Dancing elephants, performing seals, lions, clowns,
balloons, and a friendly giraffe make up a private
circus to entertain children for many years.

About Kathy Carr

As soon as Kathy Carr got the news that her sister was
going to have a baby, she set to work on this lively
afghan. "I wanted to make something special," she
says. The circus theme came to her as she was leafing
through pattern books, but the actual designs she
developed by adapting her favorite circus pictures. "I
chose these colors," she adds, "because I believe that
babies need to be stimulated with bright colors." A
mother of four, like Kathy, knows that firsthand.

SIZE: About 43″ × 62″, plus 2″ ruffle

MATERIALS: Yarn: Knitting worsted, about 28 oz Kelly green (MC), 16 oz white (W), 3½ oz each red, yellow, medium blue, black, small amounts of salmon, brown, orange, mustard, gray, rust, light blue, pale pink, natural, fuchsia, navy, and lilac; **circular knitting needle:** 36″-long size 9 (5.50 mm) *or the size that gives you the correct gauge;* **crochet hook:** size G (4.50 mm); yarn bobbins; 2 yd 45″-wide quilted fabric for backing (optional).

GAUGE: 9 sts = 2″; 11 rows = 2″.

Note: Use separate balls or bobbins for large single-color areas. Carry yarn loosely across back for areas of 4 or fewer sts. When changing colors, twist yarn to avoid holes in work, bringing the new color under the color you have been working with.

On the original afghan, the design was entirely knitted. If you find working with many colors in each row difficult, you can knit the large single-color areas, then embroider details (faces, cage bars, etc.) in duplicate stitch when knitting is completed.

PATTERN STITCH: Twisted Stockinette St. **Row 1:** Working in back loop of each st, knit across. **Row 2:** P across. Repeat these 2 rows for pattern stitch.

KNITTED PANEL: Starting at lower edge with color MC, cast on 194 sts. Do not join. Work back and forth on circular needle in twisted stockinette st throughout as follows: Work 4 rows. **Row 5:** Work 5 sts with MC, attach W and work to last 5 sts, with 2nd ball MC work 5 sts. Work with colors as established for 3 more rows. **Row 9:** Attaching new colors as needed, work 5 MC, 4 W, 35 MC, 4 W; work Chart 1 on next 98 sts as follows: starting with first row, work from A to B once, then from B back to A; work 4 W, 35 MC, 4 W, 5 MC; continue working Chart 1 on center 98 sts, keeping remaining sts in colors as established, until 16th row of Chart 1 is completed.

Next row (right side): K 5 MC, 4 W; work Chart 2 on next 35 sts as follows: starting with first row, work from A to B once; k 4 W, work next row of Chart 1 on next 98 sts, k 4 W, work Chart 2 on next 35 sts as before, k 4 W, 5 MC. Continue as established, working Chart 2 from A to B on k rows and from B to A on p rows, and working upper balloon colors as follows: with right side facing you, work Z balloon in red at beginning of row (right side edge) and in orange at end of row; work X balloon in orange at beginning of row and in red at end of row (left side edge). When Chart 2 is completed, continue on those 35 sts each side with MC until Chart 1 is completed, ending with k row.

Next row (wrong side): P 5 MC, p W to last 5 sts, p 5 MC. Work with colors as established for 3 more rows.

Next row (wrong side): P 5 MC, 4 W; work Chart 3 on next 35 sts as follows: starting with first row, work from A to B once; p 4 W, work Chart 4 on center 98 sts as follows: starting with first row, work from B to A once; p 4 W; work Chart 3 on next 35 sts as follows: starting with first row, work from B to A once. Continuing as established, work Chart 3 at right side edge from A to B on k rows and from B to A on p rows, Chart 4 from A to B on k rows and B to A on p rows, and Chart 3 at left side edge from B to A on k rows and A to B on p rows. Complete charts, ending with p row.

Next row (right side): K 5 MC, work W to last 5 sts, K 5 MC. Work with colors as established for 3 more rows.

Next row (right side): K 5 MC, 4 W, 35 MC, 4 W; work Chart 5 on center 98 sts as follows: starting with first row, work from A to B once, then from B to A once, k 4 W, 35 MC, 4 W, 5 MC. Continue working chart on center 98 sts, keeping remaining sts as established until 3rd row is completed.

Next row (wrong side): P 5 MC, 4 W; working balloon strings with black, follow Chart 2, first row, from B to A; p 4 W, continue Chart 5 on center 98 sts, p 4 W; working balloon strings with black, work Chart 2 from B to A; p 4 W, 5 MC. Continue to work as established, working Chart 2 from A to B on k rows and B to A on p rows. Work upper balloon colors same as before. Continue until Chart 2 is completed.

Next row: Work 5 MC, 4 W, 35 MC, 4 W, continue Chart 5 on center 98 sts, work 4 W, 35 MC, 4 W, 5 MC. Continue in this manner until Chart 5 is completed.

Next row: Work 5 MC, work in W to last 5 sts, work 5 MC. Work with colors as established for 3 more rows. Break off W. With MC only, work 3 rows.

Next row (right side): Starting with first row, follow Chart 6, working from A to center once, place a marker on needle, follow Chart 7 working from center to B once. Continue following Charts 6 and 7, working B to A on p rows and A to B on k rows. When Charts 6 and 7 are completed, work 4 rows with W only. Bind off all sts with W.

CROCHETED RUFFLE: Attach MC to lower right corner. **Rnd 1:** With right side of work facing you, using crochet hook, ch 3, work 2 dc in same place as joining, dc in end of every other row along right side edge to corner, work (3 dc, ch 2, 3 dc) in corner, dc in each st across top edge, work corner as before, work dc in every other row along left side edge, work corner, dc in each st across lower edge, work 3 dc in corner, ch 2, join with sl st to top of ch 3. **Rnd 2:** Ch 3, work 2 dc over ch-2, dc in each dc around, working (3 dc, ch 2, 3 dc) in each corner ch-2 sp; work 3 dc over last corner ch 2, ch 2, join to top of ch 3. Break off MC. Attach W to same corner. **Rnd 3:** With W, ch 3, * work 2 dc over ch 2, work 2 dc in each sp between 2 dc to next corner, work (3 dc, ch 2, 3 dc) in corner, dc in next 9 sp, work (2 dc in next sp, dc in next 10 sp) 17 times, 2 dc in next sp, dc in each sp to corner, work corner, 2 dc in each sp to next corner, work corner; work dc in next 9 sp, work (2 dc in next sp, dc in next 10 sp) 17 times, 2 dc in sp, dc in each sp to corner, 3 dc in corner sp, ch 2, join to top of ch 3. **Rnd 4:** Ch 3, work (dc in next 10 sp, 2 dc in next sp) around, working 6 dc in each corner ch-2 sp; join. Break off.

FINISHING (optional): Cut backing fabric 45" × 64", or 1" larger all around than knitted panel, omitting crocheted ruffle. Turn 1" under all around and, with wrong sides together, slip-stitch backing to afghan with MC. Tie layers together as follows: with thread or yarn threaded in needle, make a single stitch through backing, catching back of knitted panel without having stitch show on front. Tie ends into knot on back. Space knots about 8" apart over backing.

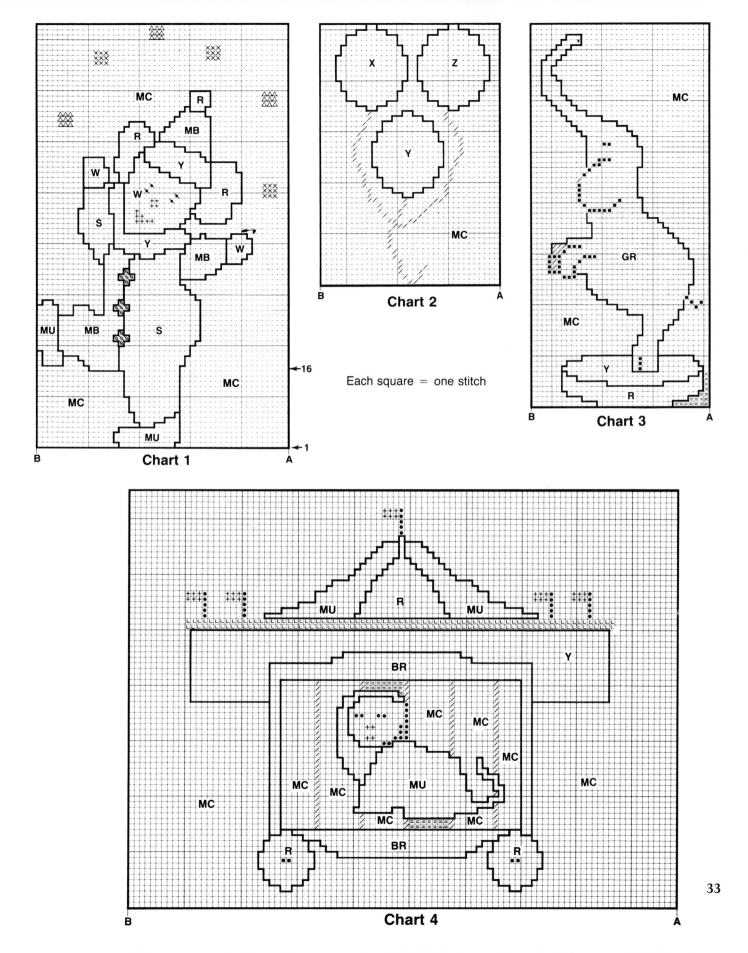

Each square = one stitch

Chart 1

Chart 2

Chart 3

Chart 4

33

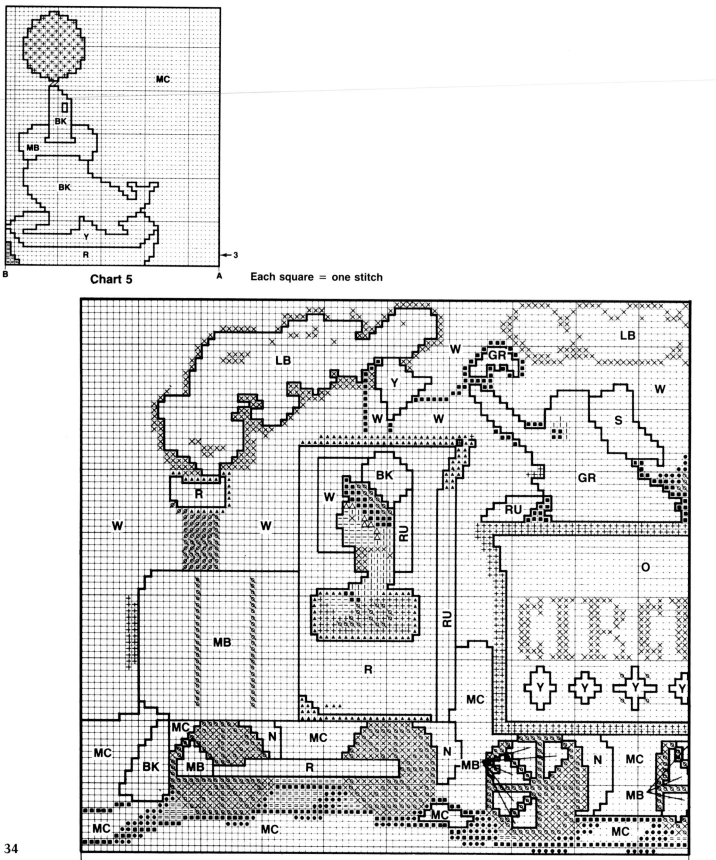

Chart 5

Each square = one stitch

Chart 7

center

B

Color Key

MC or ⊟ = kelly green   MB or ⊠ = medium blue
W or ☐ = white   LB or ⧅ = light blue
GR or ⧄ = gray   S or △ = salmon
BK or ■ = black   ⊟ = pale pink
BR or ● = brown | = natural
MU or ○ = mustard   ◐ = fuchsia
O or ⊘ = orange   L = lilac
Y or ⧄ = yellow   N = navy
R or ⊞ = red   L or X , Z (see directions)
RU or ▲ = rust

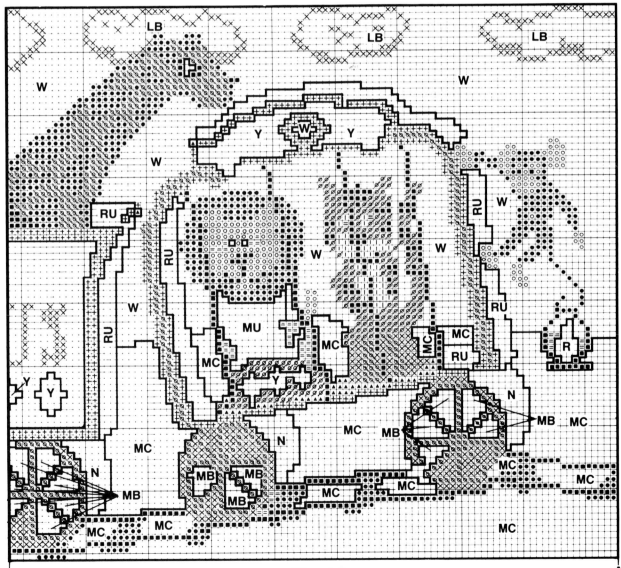

center   **Chart 6**   A

35

Flower Petals and Lace

Afghan crocheted in forty pieces by Jean Cates of
Centerville, Indiana

Single, half double, double and treble crochet stitches
produce the flower-petaled hexagons.

About Jean Cates

"The design came from a Christmas potholder,"
explains Jean Cates. "I thought it so pretty that it had
to be prettier if I used more of them." What were
originally bright reds and greens appear here as soft
peach flowers against a lacy off-white background. Jean
planned the afghan for her grandmother, who years
before had guided her through the basics of crochet.
The springtime colors, she felt, would complement the
turquoise-and-white scheme of her grandmother's
living room. When the afghan was returned to her
after her grandmother's death, she passed it on to her
daughter, for her hope chest, so it is now a family
heirloom. Jean made the afghan mostly during lunch
hours at work, where she is a quality-control reviewer
for the Indiana State Department of Public Welfare.

SIZE: About 48″ × 58″

MATERIALS: Yarn: Knitting worsted, 36 oz natural (MC), 12 oz light beige (A), 8 oz peach (B); **crochet hook:** size J (6.00 mm) *or the size that gives you the correct gauge.*

GAUGE: Each hexagon measures 7¼″ across from side to side; each diamond measures 6¼″ across from point to point.

FLOWER-PETALED HEXAGONS: Make 40. Starting at center with MC, ch 6. Join with sl st to form ring. **Rnd 1:** Ch 1, work 12 sc over ring. Join with sl st to first sc. Break off MC; attach B. **Rnd 2:** With B, ch 1, sc in first sc, ch 7, sc in 2nd ch from hook, hdc in next ch, dc in next 2 ch, hdc in next ch, sc in last ch of ch 7 (first petal made), * sc in next sc of Rnd 1, ch 7, sc in 2nd ch from hook, hdc in next ch, dc in next 2 ch, hdc in next ch, sc in last ch of ch 7 (another petal made); repeat from * around; join (12 petals). Break off B; attach A. As you work next rnd, fold petals forward, so that Rnd 3 is worked *between* and *behind* petals. **Rnd 3:** With A, ch 5, * dc in st between next 2 petals, ch 2; repeat from * around; join to 3rd ch of ch 5 (12 ch-2 loops behind petals). **Rnd 4:** With A, * ch 8, sc in 2nd ch from hook, hdc in next ch, dc in next ch, tr in next ch, dc in next ch, hdc in next ch, sc in last ch of ch 8 (leaf made), work 2 sc over next ch-2 loop, sc in next dc; repeat from * around, ending with 3 sc over last ch-2 loop; join to base of ch 8 (12 leaves). Break off A; attach MC.

On next rnd, fold leaves forward and work into sc between them. **Rnd 5:** With MC, * ch 1 (behind leaf) sc in next 3 sc between leaves; repeat from * around; join. Catch tip of B petals in work as follows on next rnd: **Rnd 6:** With MC, * sc over ch 1 behind leaf, sc in next sc, insert hook through tip of next petal and work sc in next sc (tip of petal caught in work so petal lies extended on top of work), sc in next sc; repeat from * around; join to first sc. Continue to hold leaves forward as you work next rnd. **Rnd 7:** Ch 3, dc in next 3 sc, * ch 1, dc in next 4 sc; repeat from * around, ending with ch 1; join to top of ch 3.

Catch tip of leaves in work as follows on next rnd: **Rnd 8:** Ch 3, dc in next 3 dc, * insert hook through tip of next leaf, yo and draw through leaf tip and loop on hook (ch 1 made with tip of leaf caught in work), dc in next 4

dc; repeat from * around, catching last leaf in ch; join to top of ch 3. **Rnd 9:** Ch 1, sc in top of ch 3, sc in next dc, work 3 dc in next dc (point made), * sc in next dc, sc in ch where leaf was attached, sc in next 4 dc, sc in ch, sc in next 2 dc, work 3 dc in next dc (another point made); repeat from * around, ending with sc in ch; join to first sc (6 points; 9 sc between points). **Rnd 10:** Ch 1, * sc in each sc to next point, sc in first dc of point, 3 sc in next dc, sc in next dc; repeat from * around, ending with sc in last sc; join to first sc. Break off.

LACY DIAMONDS: Make 28. Starting at center with MC, ch 6. Join to form ring. **Rnd 1:** Ch 1, work 10 sc over ring. Join to first sc. **Rnd 2:** Ch 3, dc in same sc, * 2 dc in next sc; repeat from * around; join to top of ch 3 (20 dc, counting ch 3 as first dc). **Rnd 3:** Ch 3, dc in next dc, (2 dc in next dc, dc in next 2 dc) 5 times; 2 dc in next dc, dc in next dc, 2 dc in last dc (27dc); join. **Rnd 4:** Ch 3, dc in next dc, (2 dc in next dc, dc in next 2 dc) 8 times, 2 dc in last dc (36 dc); join. **Rnd 5:** Ch 3, dc in next dc, (2 dc in next dc, dc in next 3 dc) 8 times, dc in last 2 dc (44 dc); join. **Rnd 6:** Ch 1, sc in top of ch 3, sc in next 9 dc, * work 3 dc in next dc (point made), dc in next 10 dc; repeat from * around, ending with 3 dc in last dc (4 points); join to first sc. Break off.

ASSEMBLY: See Assembly Diagram. Joining hexagons along opposite sides and leaving 2 sides unattached between joinings, make 5 strips of 8 hexagons each. Crochet pieces together on wrong side, using a sl st through front loop only. Easing shapes to fit together neatly, join side of diamonds to unattached sides of hexagon strips, crocheting edges together.

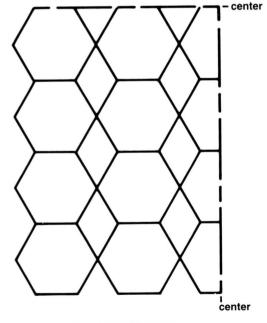

center

center

Assembly Diagram

Native American Vibrations

Spread crocheted in afghan stitch, then cross-stitched
by Jeanne Crooks of Bethel Park, Pennsylvania

The strong geometric patterns and dramatic palette of
the American Indian inspires a striking afghan.

About Jeanne Crooks

Jeanne Crooks always liked Indian designs, so she planned one just to suit herself. "My favorite color is red, and along with black, white, and turquoise, it makes a perfect Indian combination." A prolific needleworker, Jeanne works left-handed when she embroiders and right-handed when she crochets, because her mother could not teach her left-handed crochet. But her afghan stitch is self-taught. Jeanne noticed "this funny little stitch on the toe" of all the baby booties her mother made, and after her mother was gone she ripped one back to see if she could do it. It turned out to be the afghan stitch! Jeanne has won many blue ribbons for her needlework—30 or 40, she estimates. She says she has made "tons of afghans, scarves, gloves, booties, pillows, etc. (You can do a lot of crocheting in seventy-three years.)" Despite this volume, she never sells her work, but prefers to give it away to the "people I love."

SIZE: About 58" × 67", plus 7½" fringed border

MATERIALS: Yarn: Knitting worsted, 72 oz bright red (color R), 16 oz black (B), 7 oz each white (W) and turquoise (T); **afghan hook:** size I (5.50 mm) *or the size that gives you the correct gauge;* **crochet hook:** size I; tapestry needle.

GAUGE: 7 sts = 2"; 7 rows = 2". Each strip is 14¼" wide.

PATTERN STITCH: Plain Afghan Stitch. See Plain Afghan Stitch, page 195.

STRIP: Make 4. With color R, ch 51. Work in plain afghan st on 50 sts for 17 rows; break off. Attach B, work 15 rows; break off. Attach R, work 167 rows; break off. Attach B, work 15 rows; break off. Attach R, work 16 rows. Sl st in each st across. Break off.

ASSEMBLY: Neatly weave together side edges of 4 strips, matching rows.

EMBROIDERY: See Cross-Stitch over Afghan Stitch, page 195. Embroider Center Design between black bands as follows: start at right edge of first R row above black bands and, following first row of Chart 1, work across row, repeating from X to Z (at seam) 3 times, then from X to Y once. You may find it easier to work B outlines first, then fill in areas as indicated, leaving R areas as unworked red background. Repeat Chart 1 in length from A to C once, then from A to B once, ending on last R row before black band.

Embroider Border Design on bottom red band as follows: start at right edge on 7th row of band and, following 2nd row of Chart 2, work across red band, * repeating from W to X 5 times, then W to Z once, ending at seam; repeat from * 3 times more, ending last repeat at Y (left edge). Complete chart. Turn afghan upside down and work Border Design on top red band to correspond.

BORDER: Attach B to edge of afghan and with crochet hook work 3 rows of sc around afghan, working 3 sc in center st at each corner on each row. Work fringed border across each end of afghan as follows: **Next row:** Attach B to corner. * Ch 5, skip 2 sc, sc in next sc; repeat from * across. Ch 5, turn. **Next row:** Sc in 3rd ch of first ch 5, * ch 5, sc in 3rd ch of next ch 5; repeat from * across, ending with ch 5, sl st to base of first ch 5 of previous row.

FRINGE: See Fringes, page 196. For each fringe cut one 20″ strand of each color. Tie fringe in center of each ch-5 loop of last row across one end. Separate fringe strands into 2 groups, with a strand of each color in each group. Tie a knot in first group of first fringe 1″ below where fringe was attached. * Knot together 2nd group of same fringe with first group of next fringe 1″ below where fringes were attached. Repeat from * across row, ending with knot in 2nd group of last fringe. Trim fringe ends evenly. Make fringe across other end in same manner.

Color Key

⊡ = red background (R) (unworked)

☒ = black (B)

▯ = white (W)

▢ = turquoise (T)

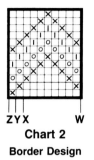

Chart 2
Border Design

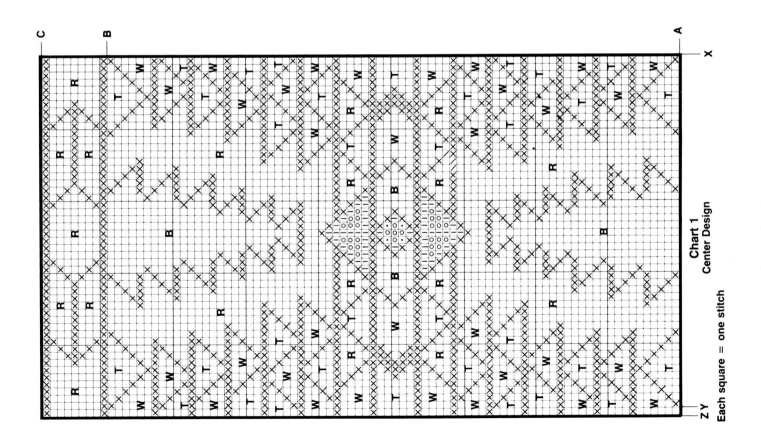

Chart 1
Center Design

Each square = one stitch

43

Royal Stewart Plaid

An easy project, crocheted and woven by
Marion Currie of Inglewood, Ontario

The secret here is filet crochet, forming a base for the
stripes woven in with a tapestry needle.

About Marion Currie

Marion Currie's afghan was a shower present, made to
please the girl who married her son's best friend.
When the girl, named Stewart, came to visit the
Curries, she asked Marion if she could crochet an
afghan in the Royal Stewart plaid. "I will say it was an
enjoyable challenge," says Marion, "and we were very
happy when we accomplished what we set out to do."
But it actually took Marion and her son, working from
a length of Royal Stewart material, thirty to forty hours
to plot the colors and the size of the pattern blocks in
the correct proportion. Another hundred hours went
into finishing the job. Days are busy on the small
Canadian farm where Marion and her husband raise
peacocks and pheasants, and "when I sit down in the
evening," she says, "I find knitting and crocheting
very relaxing."

SIZE: About 60″ × 76″, plus 6″ fringe at each end

MATERIALS: Yarn: Knitting worsted, 45½ oz bright red (color A), 14 oz navy (B), 8 oz green (C), 6 oz medium blue (D), 4 oz each yellow (E) and white (F); **crochet hook:** size G (4.50 mm) *or the size that gives you the correct gauge;* large-eyed tapestry needle.

GAUGE: 2 meshes = 1″; 9 rows = 4″.

Note: This afghan is made by first crocheting a filet mesh foundation with horizontal stripes, then weaving yarn, threaded into tapestry needle, through spaces to form vertical stripes.

MESH FOUNDATION: Starting at one end with color D, ch 240. **Row 1:** Work dc in 6th ch from hook (first sp made), *ch 1, skip next ch, dc in next ch (another sp made); repeat from * across (118 sp). Break off D; attach A. Ch 4, turn. **Row 2:** Skip first dc, * dc in next dc, ch 1; repeat from * across, ending with dc in last dc, ch 1, skip 1 ch of turning ch, dc in next ch of turning ch (118 sp). Ch 4, turn. Repeat Row 2 for pattern of 118 sp on each row throughout, working horizontal stripes as follows: work 19 more rows A, * then work 1 row D, 2 B, 1 E, 1 B, 1 F, 1 B, 3 C, 2 A, 1 B, 1 A, 1 F, 1 A, 1 B, 2 A, 3 C, 1 B, 1 F, 1 B, 1 E, 2 B, 1 D (horizontal stripe made), then work 20 rows of A; repeat from * twice more, then work 1 row D. Do not break off; work side edging as follows: turn work sideways to crochet a row of sc with D along side edge, working 2 sc over each end dc or turning ch. Break off. Attach D to opposite-side edge at corner and crochet a row of sc in same manner. Break off D. Attach A to any corner. Crochet a row of sc all around afghan, working 3 sc at each corner and working each A sc into back of D st (inserting hook into work behind st), leaving top 2 loops of each D st unworked to form chain st on right side of work.

WOVEN VERTICAL STRIPES: *Note:* Work with double strand of yarn threaded into large-eyed tapestry needle. Cut yarn lengths long enough (about 92″) to weave through sp with 7″ length extending at each end for fringe. Keep yarn strands flat and untwisted as you weave, keeping strands just loose enough to keep filet foundation from rippling.

    Hold work sideways to work along one side (long)

edge with double strand of A, weaving needle in first sp, out the next sp along edge to end, leaving 7" lengths at each end. In next row of sp, bring needle *up* from wrong side through first sp, into the next sp, out next sp, along row to opposite end, so that yarn strands alternate in and out with previous row to resemble weaving. Continue to alternate weaving of strands in this manner, working until 20 rows of A are completed, * then work stripe rows in same color sequence as for horizontal stripes of foundation, work 20 rows of A; repeat from * once more, ending along opposite-side edge of afghan.

FRINGE: See Fringes, page 196. Make fringe along each narrow end of afghan by tying yarn ends of every 4 rows together in overhand knot. Trim ends of fringe evenly.

Fan Dance

A second-prize winner, designed and crocheted by
Katherine Marianne Eng of San Francisco, California

Vibrant fans dance to the timeless rhythm of an Amish
quilt pattern.

About Katherine Marianne Eng

When she was just a child, Katherine Eng made
potholders by the dozen to give as Christmas gifts.
Then she lost interest in crocheting, and didn't take it
up again until her early twenties. At that point she
worked as a dancer in Las Vegas and needed something
to do backstage while waiting for her calls. Between
working as a professional dancer for ten years and
being a mother and homemaker, she made and sold
dresses to boutiques, crocheted sweaters for a knit-wear
designer, and (four years ago, with her artist and art-
teacher husband) hosted a Christmas Craft Fair. "I don't
get along well with microwaves, computers, or even
sewing machines," says Katherine. "I consider myself
a rather old-fashioned person—kind of a pioneer
trapped in the modern world." So, much as she loves
quilts, she prefers to crochet, not sew them. She designed
and made this afghan for the *Woman's Day* contest,
using quilt books for inspiration and avoiding complex
crochet stitches that might in any way detract from the
vibrant colors and bold design of her entry.

SIZE: About 57" × 65"

MATERIALS: Yarn: Knitting worsted, 35 oz black (MC) in different dye lots to give subtle varied effect, 18 oz skipper blue (color A), 7 oz each medium blue (B) and navy (C), 3½ oz each (or scraps of varied colors) turquoise, amethyst, dark rose, lavender, navy, hyacinth, violet, vermilion, forest green, teal, light teal, smoky blue, moss green, and claret; **crochet hook:** size G (4.50 mm) *or the size that gives you the correct gauge;* tapestry needle.

GAUGE: 9 sts = 2". Each block measures about 7½" square.

BLOCK: Make 30. **Fan:** Work each fan with a different combination of 9 colors, excluding MC, as follows: starting at one side edge of fan, ch 16. **Row 1 (right side):** Sc in 2nd ch from hook and in next 4 ch, hdc in next 5 ch, dc in last 5 ch (15 sts). Ch 3, turn. **Row 2:** Skip first dc, dc in next 4 dc, hdc in next 5 hdc, sc in next 5 sc. Cut color in use; join new color; ch 1, turn. *Note:* As you work, enclose cut ends in sts. **Row 3:** Sc in first 5 sc, hdc in next 5 hdc, dc in last 4 dc, dc in top of turning ch. Ch 3, turn. Repeating Rows 2 and 3, work until 18 rows (9 colored 2-row wedges) have been completed. Fasten off. **Fan Edging:** With right side of work facing you, join A where you fastened off, work 3 sc in same st (corner made), sc in next 13 sts, work 3-sc corner in top of turning ch; work 35 sc evenly spaced along curved upper edge (working about 2 sc for each row); work corner in corner st, sc in next 13 ch of starting edge, work corner in last ch; work 16 sc evenly spaced across lower edge; join with sl st to first sc. Fasten off.

Shape upper corner of block: With right side of fan facing you, join MC to center st on first corner of upper edge. **Row 1:** Ch 3, work 2 dc in same corner st, skip next 2 sts, sc in next st, * skip next st, work shell (2 dc, ch 2, 2 dc) in next st, skip next st, sc in next st; repeat from * 7 times more, skip next 2 sts, work 3 dc in corner st. Ch 1, turn. **Row 2:** Sc in first dc, skip 2 dc, work 3 dc in next sc, sc in next ch-2 sp, work (shell in next sc, sc in next ch-2 sp) 7 times, work 3 dc in next sc, sc in top of ch 3. Turn. **Row 3:** Sl st to next ch-2 sp, sl st in sp, skip 2 dc, work 2 dc in next sc, work (sc in next ch-2 sp, shell in next sc) 4 times, sc in next ch-2 sp, 2 dc in next sc, sl st in last ch-2 sp. Turn. **Row 4:** Sl st to first ch-2 sp, sl st in sp, work (shell in next sc, sc in next ch-2 sp) 3 times. Turn. **Row 5:** Sl st to first ch-2 sp, sc in same sp, work (shell in next sc, sc in next ch-2 sp) twice. Turn. **Row 6:** Sl st to first ch-2 sp, sc in sp, work (3 dc, ch 2, 3 dc) all in next sc, sc in next ch-2 sp. Fasten off.

Shape lower corner of block: With right side of work facing you, join MC to center st of first corner at lower edge of fan. **Row 1:** Sc in corner st; draw up loop in each of next 2 sc, yo and draw through all 3 loops on hook (sc dec made); sc across, decreasing 6 more sts evenly spaced and ending with sc in corner (13 sc). Ch 3, turn. **Row 2:** Dc in first sc, skip 1 sc, sc in next sc, work (skip 1 sc, shell in next sc, skip 1 sc, sc in next sc) twice, skip 1 sc, 2 dc in last sc. Ch 1, turn. **Row 3:** Sc in first dc, 2 dc in next sc, sc in next ch-2 sp, shell in next sc, sc in next ch-2 sp, 2 dc in next sc, sc in top of ch 3. Ch 1, turn. **Row 4:** Sc in next dc, 3 dc in next sc, sc in next ch-2 sp, 3 dc in next sc, sc in last sc. Ch 1, turn. **Row 5:** Sc in next dc, work (3 dc, ch 2, 3 dc) in next sc, sc in last sc. Fasten off.

ASSEMBLY: Arrange blocks, right side up, following Placement Diagram. Sew together with MC.

BORDER: Rnd 1: With right side facing you and starting near center of one edge with A, work an odd number of sc evenly spaced on each edge of afghan, working (sc, ch 2, sc) at each corner; join to first sc. Ch 1, turn. **Rnd 2:** Sc in same sc as joining, ch 1, * skip 1 sc, sc in next sc, ch 1; repeat from * around, working (sc, ch 2, sc, ch 1) in each corner sp; join. Ch 1, turn. **Rnd 3:** * Sc in next sp, ch 1, skip next sc; repeat from * around, working corners as before; join. Ch 1, turn. **Rnds 4 through 6:** Repeat Rnd 3 three times more. Cut A; join B, ch 1, turn. **Rnd 7:** With B, * sc in next ch-1 sp, dc in next sc; repeat from * around, working (sc, ch 2, sc) in each corner sp; join. Ch 3, turn. **Rnd 8:** * Sc in next sc, dc in next dc; repeat from * around, working (dc, ch 2, dc) at corners; join. Ch 3, turn. **Rnd 9:** Repeat Rnd 8, working (sc, ch 2, sc) at corners. Cut B; join A, ch 3, turn. **Rnd 10:** With A, dc in each st around, working (dc, ch 3, dc) at each corner; join. Ch 1, turn. **Rnd 11:** Sc in each st around, working (sc, ch 3, sc) at each corner; join. Cut A; join MC, ch 1, turn. **Rnd 12:** With MC, sc in first sc, * skip 2 sc, work (2 dc, ch 2, 2 dc) in next sc, skip next 2 sc, sc in next sc; repeat from * around, working (3 dc, ch 2, 3 dc) at corners and adjusting number

Placement Diagram

of sts skipped near corners, if necessary, so shell pattern will repeat smoothly; join. Turn. **Rnd 13:** Sl st in first sc, work (ch 3, dc, ch 2, 2 dc) in same sc (first shell made), sc in next ch-2 sp, * work (2 dc, ch 2, 2 dc) in next sc, sc in next ch-2 sp; repeat from * around and at corners, working sc in 2nd dc before corner sp, work (3 dc, ch 2, 3 dc) in corner sp, skip 1 dc, then sc in next dc; end rnd with sl st in top of ch 3. Turn. **Rnds 14 through 24:** Repeat Rnd 13 eleven times more. Cut MC; join C, ch 1, turn. **Rnd 25 (right side):** With C, sc in first sc, * sc in next 2 dc, work (sc, ch 2, sc) in next sp, sc in next 2 dc, sc in next sc; repeat from * around, working sc in 3 dc each side of each corner sp and (sc, ch 3, sc) in corner sp; join. Fasten off C; turn. **Rnd 26:** With A, ** work (sc, ch 2, sc, ch 5, sc, ch 2, sc) in a corner sp, ch 3, skip 4 sc, * sc in next sc, ch 3, work (sc, ch 2, sc) in next ch-2 sp, ch 3, skip 3 sc; repeat from * to next corner sp, skip 4 sc; repeat from ** 3 times more; join. Fasten off.

Weave 1 strand of C, threaded in tapestry needle, through spaces of Rnd 2, under and over sts of Rnds 8 and 11. With A, embroider 3 lazy-daisy stitches (see Embroidery Stitches, page 203) over first, center, and last dc at each corner of Rnd 12.

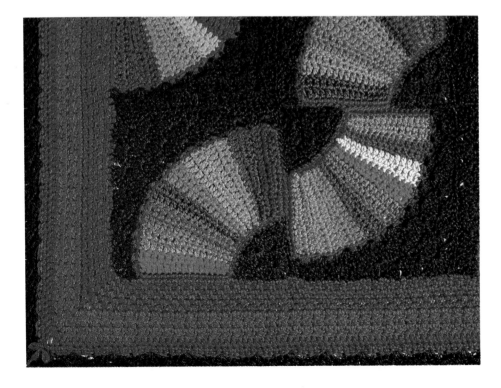

Rainbow Ripples

A third-prize winner, crocheted by Barbara Farrall of Rochelle, Illinois

This fabulous afghan would energize any bedroom.

About Barbara Farrall

Although Barbara Farrall's coverlet, with its spirited colors and stark white background, is most contemporary in feeling, Barbara says, "It is actually from an old-time pattern I remember my grandmother crocheting." Barbara also confides that the hard part was thinking out the pattern for herself and reworking it until it was correct, and that the colors were not of her choosing. "I began with some earth tones, duller colors. When my husband, Ross, saw the first few rows he suggested more cheerful colors. I changed, and I'm glad I did! My husband is a big inspiration in my needlecrafting, because he supports me totally."

SIZE: About 70" × 85"

MATERIALS: Yarn: Knitting worsted, 108 oz white (MC), about 5 oz each red (A), yellow (B), and green (C), 3 oz blue (D); **crochet hook:** size J (6.00 mm) *or the size that gives you the correct gauge.*

GAUGE: 3 meshes = 2½"; 3 rows = 3".

NOTE: Rounds of stand-up dc are worked over a mesh (filet) foundation to create the three-dimensional ripple design.

MESH FOUNDATION: Starting at one long edge with MC, ch 202. **Row 1:** Dc in 6th ch from hook, * ch 1, skip next ch, dc in next ch; repeat from * across (99 spaces). Ch 4, turn. **Row 2:** * Dc in next dc, ch 1; repeat from * across, ending with skip 1 ch of turning ch, dc in next ch. Ch 4, turn. Repeat Row 2 for 67 more rows (69 rows worked). Fasten off.

RIPPLE PATTERN: *Note:* Start first rnd of ripples at outer edge, working each following rnd in toward center. Work in rnds facing outer edge (front of sts face you and inside of afghan; back of sts face outer edge). **Rnd 1:** Join A around st at top right corner sp on mesh base (see first arrow at beginning of Rnd 1 on Ripple Stitch Diagram; note that diagram does not represent the whole afghan, but only the procedure for this stitch), ch 3 (count as first dc), dc around same st on base; following direction of arrows, * work 2 dc around st on left side of sp, 2 dc around st at bottom of next sp, 2 dc around st on left side; work 2 dc around st at top of next sp; repeat from * around, working 2 dc on each side of corners; end with 2 dc in last corner; join in top of ch 3. Fasten off. **Rnd 2:** Following diagram, join MC around st at left side of first empty sp in a corner, ch 3, dc around same st, * 2 dc around st at top of next sp, work 2 dc around st at left side, 2 dc around st at bottom of next sp, and 2 dc around st at left side; repeat from * around, working along corners as shown in diagram: join. Fasten off. **Rnd 3:** Join MC around st at right side of corner sp, ch 3 and dc around same st, then continue as before, working corners as for Rnd 1. Repeating Rnds 2 and 3 for pattern st, continue with 3 more rnds MC, 1 rnd B, 5 MC, 1 C, 5 MC, 1 D, 5 MC, 1 A, 1 MC, 1 B, 1 MC, 1 C, 1 MC, 1 D, 1 MC (32 rnds). Follow Center Panel Chart, working squares 1 through 4 (center

square), then continue with squares 3, 2, and 1 to complete panel of seven squares.

BORDER: Rnd 1: With right side of work facing you, using MC, work 3 dc and ch 2 in each empty sp on outer edge, working (3 dc, ch 2, 3 dc) between 2nd and 3rd dc at corners; join. **Rnd 2:** Ch 3, * sc in next sp, ch 3, 3 dc in same sp; repeat from * around; join. Fasten off.

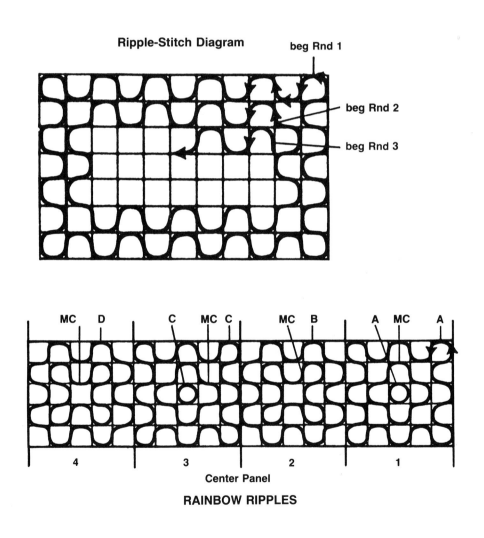

Ripple-Stitch Diagram

beg Rnd 1

beg Rnd 2

beg Rnd 3

MC D C MC C MC B A MC A

4 3 2 1

Center Panel

RAINBOW RIPPLES

Canadian Evergreens

A crocheted throw (also suitable for hanging) by
June Forrester of Campbell River, British Columbia

A skillful use of braiding helps frame the scene, while
twisted chain loops subtly but surely delineate the
trunks of the evergreens.

About June Forrester

With simplicity, economy, and great charm, June
Forrester's afghan captures the essential majesty of the
landscape in British Columbia. Whether you view
it as a native or a tourist, it recalls the striking
natural beauty of Canada's western province: vast
unbroken vistas punctuated with tall straight
evergreens, sparkling with crystalline lakes, stretching
under the clear, bright abundant sky. June lives with
her husband and one of her two daughters on a
wooded one-acre property, beautifully landscaped with
shrubs and flowers. Although a needleworker since
childhood, June says this is her first try at designing.

SIZE: About 40″ × 66″

MATERIALS: Yarn: Knitting worsted, 28 oz burnt orange for border (color A) 21 oz forest green (F), 11 oz gold (G), 12 oz sky blue (SB), 8 oz light olive (LO), and 4 oz each plum (P), white (W), coral (C), and beige (B); **crochet hook:** size J (6.00 mm) *or the size that gives you the correct gauge.*

GAUGE: 3 sts = 1″; 10 rows of alternating dc and sc = 4″.

AFGHAN: Starting at lower edge of afghan, with border, ch 190 with color A. **Row 1 (right side):** Dc in 4th ch from hook and in each remaining ch (188 dc, counting first ch 3 as a dc). Piece should measure about 63″ long. Ch 3, turn. **Row 2:** Work a long dc around post of next dc as follows: leaving 2 loops unworked at top of dc, yo and insert hook horizontally from front to back to front again behind post of dc, yo and draw up a loop, (yo and draw through 2 loops on hook) twice—long dc made with ridge formed on right side of work by unworked top of previous dc row; work long dc around post of each dc across; dc in top of turning ch 3. Ch 3, turn. **Row 3:** Start border stitch patterns. Skip first dc, dc in next 4 dc, * work long dc as before around post of next dc, dc in next 2 dc, skip 1 dc, work cluster st in next dc as follows: around post of dc work (yo and draw up a loop, yo and draw through first 2 loops on hook) 3 times, yo and draw through all 4 loops on hook—cluster st made; then dc in next 2 dc, around post of last dc just worked make cluster st as before, dc in next 2 dc, work (long dc around next dc, dc in next 5 dc) twice; repeat from * 7 times more, then work long dc around next dc, dc in next 2 dc, skip 1 dc, work cluster st around next dc, dc in next 2 dc, work cluster st around post of last dc worked, dc in next 2 dc, long dc around next dc, dc in next 4 dc, dc in top of ch 3. Ch 1, turn. **Row 4 and all wrong-side rows:** Sc in each st across, sc in top of ch 3. Ch 3, turn. **Row 5:** Skip first sc, dc in next 4 sc, * long dc around post of long dc below next sc, skip unworked sc behind long dc, dc in next 2 sc, work braid on next 4 sts as follows: skip next sc, work cluster st around post of dc below next sc, work dc in unworked sc behind cluster st just completed, dc in next sc, work cluster st around post of dc below last sc just worked, skip next sc—4-st braid made; dc in next 2 sc, (work long dc below next sc, skip unworked sc behind long dc, dc in next 5 dc) twice; repeat from * 7 times more, then work

Chain Twist Diagram

long dc, 2 dc, 4-st braid, 2 dc, long dc, 5 dc. Ch 1, turn. Repeat Rows 4 and 5 five times more. Repeat Row 4.

Row 17: Work in pattern across first 21 sts, ending with long dc, then dc in next 146 sc, then, starting with long dc, work in pattern as established across last 21 sts. Ch 1, turn. Now start center design panel. **Row 18:** Sc in first 21 sts; attach G and work sc around post of next 146 dc, forming ridge on right side of work; attach another strand of A and sc in last 20 sts, sc in top of ch 3. Ch 3, turn. Continuing to work first and last 21 sts in pattern as established with A, work design on center 146 sts as follows: **Row 1:** Following Row 1 of chart from X to Y, work dc in first 20 sc, (ch 10, skip next sc, dc in next 20 sc) 6 times. Leave ch-10 loops unattached until Row 11. **Row 2:** Working row 2 of chart from Y to X, sc in first 20 dc, (ch 10, sc in next 20 dc) 6 times. Repeat Rows 1 and 2 three times more. **Row 9:** With LO, dc in first 20 sc, work (another dc in same sc as last dc worked, dc in next 20 sc) 6 times. **Row 10:** Sc in each dc across. Ch 3, turn. Now attach ch-10 loops to form tree trunk as follows: on right side of work, starting with ch-10 of Row 1 for first trunk, twist ch-10 to form loop (see Chain Twist Diagram). In same manner twist next ch-10 directly above and draw this loop through previous one. Continue in this manner, drawing each new loop through loop of previous row below until all loops of each trunk have been drawn through. The last loop at top of each trunk will be attached as you work Row 11. *Note:* To change colors within a row, work to last st of old color and, before drawing through last 2 loops of last st, drop old color on wrong side of work and complete st with new yarn. Do not carry color not in use across work, but use a separate ball of yarn for each color area. **Row 11:** With LO work dc in first 11 sc, with F work popcorn in next sc as follows: work 5 dc in next sc, drop loop from hook, insert hook through top of first dc of 5-dc group, pick up dropped loop and draw through first dc, ch 1 to fasten (popcorn made); with F, (dc in next sc, popcorn in next sc) 4 times, now attach last ch-10 loop of tree trunk below by working yo, then inserting hook front to back through loop and working dc in next sc (loop attached in dc); work popcorn in next sc, (dc in next sc, popcorn in next sc) 4 times; * with LO, dc in next 2 sc; with F, work popcorn in next sc, (dc in next sc, popcorn in next sc) 4 times, attach ch-10 loop of tree trunk below in dc worked in next sc, work popcorn in next sc, (dc in next sc, popcorn in next sc) 4 times; repeat from * 4 times more; with LO, work dc in last 11 sc. Continue following chart from X to Y on dc rows and from Y to X on sc rows, changing colors as indicated and working all F trees with popcorns same as for first tree. Complete chart (last row is dc row). Break off SB.

Work with A only. Establish border stitch pattern as follows: **Row 1:** Sc in first 21 sts, work sc around post of next 146 dc, forming ridge on right side of work, sc in last 20 sts, sc in top of ch 3. Ch 3, turn. **Row 2:** Work first 21 sts as established, dc in next 8 sc, (establish braid on next 4 sts as follows: work cluster st in next sc, dc in next 2 sc, work cluster st in same sc as last dc was worked, skip next sc; then dc in next 17 sc) 6 times, establish braid on next 4 sts as before, dc in next 8 sc, work last 21 sts as established. Ch 1, turn. **Row 3:** Sc in each st across. Ch 3, turn. **Row 4:** Work first 21 sts as established, dc in next 5 sc, * work long dc below next sc, dc in next 2 sc, work 4-st braid same as at beginning of row, dc in next 2 sc, (work long dc below next sc, dc in next 5 sc) twice; repeat from * 6 times more, completing row as established. Work as established until 13 border A rows above center design area are completed, ending with an sc row. **Row 14:** Dc in each sc across. Ch 3, turn.

Color and Stitch Key

W = white
P = plum
SB = sky blue
B = beige
C = coral
LO = light olive
F = forest green
G = gold
⚡ = ch-10 in gold
☒ = forest green
▣ = popcorn in forest green

Each square = one stitch

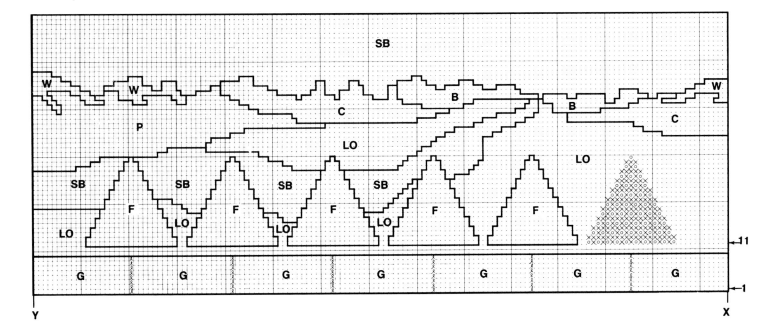

Garden Pathways

A throw designed as a quick crochet project by
Nancy Fuller of Rexford, New York

Color makes this afghan a dazzler. The designer's
techniques also make it a winner with crocheters who
like to see fast results.

About Nancy Fuller

If you always have heaps of scrap yarn around, like
Nancy Fuller, then follow her lead and develop a rich
and varied garden afghan of your own. Says Nancy, "I
love to garden, so the idea of representing a formal
garden, with hedges, paths, and multicolored beds of
blossoms, came naturally." Nancy completed her project
in about a week. By working each new flower into the
petals of an existing row, she eliminated the need to sew
all the small separate units together at the end. Another
of Nancy's timesavers was not bothering to block the
piece: "I liked the way the flower petals cupped."

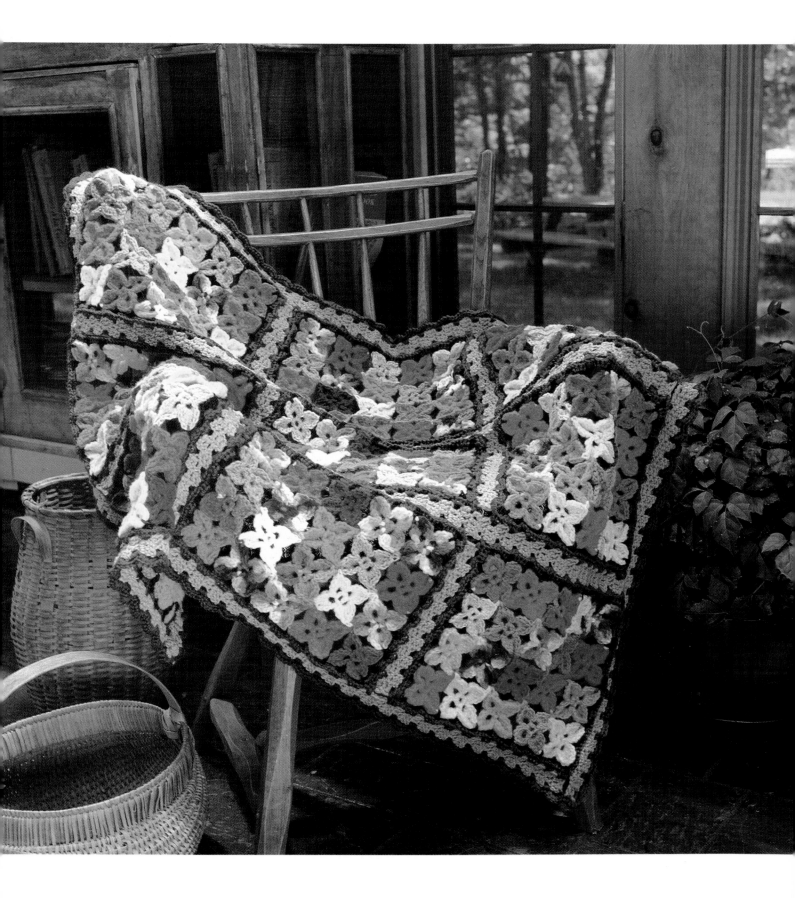

SIZE: About 34″ × 41″

MATERIALS: Yarn: Knitting worsted, 6 oz each medium gray (color A; for a more neutral effect, you may want to substitute an off-white) and forest green (B), 3 oz black (C), small amounts of assorted bright colors for flowers; **crochet hook:** size G (4.50 mm) *or the size needed to give you the correct gauge.*

GAUGE: Each flower measures about 2¼″ across. Each block of 20 flowers measures about 9″ × 11″.

Note: Work flower blocks with many different colors so that no two adjoining flowers are the same color and colors within each block are placed to give a balanced and pleasing effect.

FLOWER BLOCK: Make 9 blocks. **First strip: first flower:** starting at center with a bright flower color, ch 5. Join with sl st to form ring. **Rnd 1:** Work (sc over ring, ch 3) 4 times. Join with sl st to first sc. **Rnd 2:** Over first ch-3 loop work (sc, hdc, dc, tr, ch 1, tr, dc, hdc, sc) for petal; work petal over each remaining ch-3 loop (4 petals made). Join with sl st to first sc. Break off. **2nd flower:** See Joining Diagram. Work same as first flower until 2 petals are completed (a and b), over next ch-3 loop work (sc, hdc, dc, tr), then hold first flower behind 2nd flower, wrong sides together, sc over ch 1 at tip of a first-flower petal, attaching flowers, then work (tr, dc, hdc, sc) over same ch-3 loop of 2nd flower to complete petal, on last ch-3 loop work (sc, hdc, dc, tr), then sc over ch 1 at tip of next petal on first flower, complete petal on 2nd flower. Join to first sc and break off. **3rd flower:** Work same as first flower to tip of 3rd petal (c), then, holding 2nd flower behind 3rd flower, wrong sides together, attach flowers by working sc over ch-1 loop of next free petal of 2nd flower, complete petal on 3rd flower, work first half of next petal, attach with sc in last free petal of 2nd flower, complete petal on 3rd flower. Join and break off. Three flowers are joined in strip. Work 4th and 5th flowers in same manner to form 5-flower strip.

2nd strip: 6th flower: Work to tip of 2nd petal (b), attach to first flower by working sc at tip of same petal where 2nd flower was joined, complete 2nd petal of 6th flower, work first half of next petal, attach to next free petal of first flower, complete 6th flower. Join and break off. *Note:* On first flower, one petal remains free for corner of block; opposite petal has 2 sc worked in same place.

7th flower: Work to tip of 2nd petal (b), attach by working sc at petal tip of 2nd flower, work to tip of 3rd petal of 7th flower, attach to petal of first flower (3 sc worked into petal at corner), work to tip of 4th petal of 7th flower, attach to next free petal of 6th flower, complete 7th flower. Work 8th, 9th, and 10th flowers in same manner. Join 2 more 5-flower strips in same manner to form block of 20 flowers.

BORDER: Attach color C to corner of block at tip of flower petal. With right side of work facing you, working around edge of block, work sc over ch-1 loop of same petal, * ch 6, then, reaching behind, work dc into next sc between flower petals, ch 6, sc at next flower joining; repeat from * around, working into free petal at each corner, ending with ch 6, sl st to first sc. Break off. There are 8 ch-6 loops along each end and 10 loops along each side of block.

JOINING STRIPS: Starting at one end with A, ch 6. **Row 1:** Dc in 4th ch from hook, dc in remaining 2 ch (4 dc, counting ch 3 as first st). Ch 3, turn. **Row 2:** Skip first dc, dc in next 2 dc, dc in top of ch 3. Ch 3, turn. Repeat Row 2 for length of strips. Make 6 small strips (X on Assembly Diagram) each 16 rows long (about 9"); make 2 medium strips (Y) each 62 rows long (about 34"); make 4 long strips (Z) each 68 rows long (about 38").

ASSEMBLY: Following Assembly Diagram, lay out flower blocks, placing X strips between ends of blocks, Z strips between sides of blocks and at sides of afghan, and Y strips across top and bottom of afghan.

Join X strips to blocks as follows: attach B to corner sc of Block 1 at arrow. With right side of work facing you, work 3 sc over first ch-6 loop of block, then to attach X strip skip first row of strip, work 3 dc over end dc of next row on strip, * work 3 dc over next ch-6 loop on block, skip next row on X strip, work 3 dc over end dc of next row on strip; repeat from * to next corner, ending with 3 dc over last row of strip. Break off. Attach B to corner sc of Block 2 at arrow. Work 3 dc over end dc of first row (skipped row on previous joining) of X strip, work 3 dc over first ch-6 loop on Block 2, * skip next row of strip, work 3 dc over end dc of next row on strip, work 3 dc over next ch-6 loop on block; repeat from * to next corner, ending with 3 dc over last ch-6 loop. Break off. Join Block

3 below Block 2 in same manner. Make 2 more strips of 3 blocks with X joining strips.

Attach Z strips to blocks as follows: attach B to top left corner of a Z strip. With right side of work facing you, * work 3 dc over ch-6 loop on Block 1 at dot, skip 1 row on Z strip, work 3 dc over end dc of next row; repeat from * to next corner, ending with 3 dc over end dc, sc over next loop (first loop after corner), sc in corner of X strip between blocks, sc over end dc of next row on Z strip. Break off. Attach B to next corner of X strip, skip 2 rows of Z strip, work 3 dc over end dc of next row, work 3 dc over next loop of Block 2; continue working in same manner as before to complete attaching Blocks 2 and 3 to long strip. Attach remaining Z strips in same manner. Attach Y strips to top and bottom of afghan in same manner.

FINISHING: Attach B to lower left corner of afghan. **Row 1:** With right side of work facing you and working across edge of bottom strip, work 3 sc over end dc of first row, * ch 3, skip 1 row, work 3 sc over end dc of next row; repeat from * around afghan, working 3 sc at each corner. Join to first sc. **Row 2:** Work sc in next sc, * work 5 sc over next ch-3 loop, sc in center sc of next 3-sc group; repeat from * around. Break off.

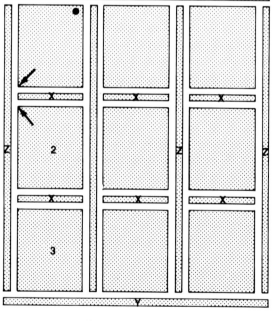

Assembly Diagram

Stitch Key

a = 1st petal worked

b = 2nd petal worked

c = 3rd petal worked

d = 4th petal worked

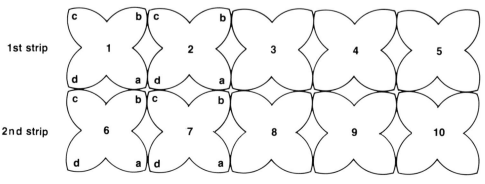

Joining Diagram

Grape Trellis

Crocheted coverlet, an easy project by Jewel Gotelli
of Healdsburg, California

Grapes in rich shades of blue and purple take their
sheen from the brushed yarns the designer uses.

About Jewel Gotelli

"We live in the heart of Sonoma County's premium
wine country," says Jewel Gotelli. "I only have to look
out the window for inspiration." But finding a pattern
for an afghan with a grape motif was another matter.
After combing through innumerable books, Jewel decided to "take a stab" at creating her own design. Her
result is both dramatic and easy to work. When Jewel
isn't crocheting she stays busy tending a summer vegetable
garden, oil painting, or sewing. "Self-taught and not an
expert at anything!" she describes herself. "Enjoying
retirement and grandkids and neighborkids and trying
to teach them to appreciate the joys of creativity."

SIZE: About 64" square

MATERIALS: Yarn: Bulky-weight brushed acrylic yarn, 51 oz pale yellow (color A), 12 oz white (B), 6 oz gray (C), 9 oz wine (D), 6 oz light maroon (E), 9 oz medium blue (F), 6 oz light blue (G), and 12 oz leaf green (H); **crochet hook:** size G (4.50 mm) *or the size that gives you the correct gauge;* tapestry needle.

GAUGE: 7 sc = 2"; 3 rows = 1". Each square block measures about 16" diagonally.

TRIANGULAR BLOCKS: Make 6. With A, ch 47. **Row 1:** Work sc in 2nd ch from hook and in each remaining ch across (46 sc). Ch 2, turn. **Row 2:** Working in back loop only, skip first sc, sc in each sc across to last sc, skip last sc (2 sc dec on row). Ch 2, turn. Repeat Row 2 until 2 sc remain. Ch 1, turn. **Next row:** Draw up a loop in each sc, yo and draw through all loops on hook (side edges of block are saw-toothed). Do not break off, but crochet a row of sc evenly spaced all around edge of block, making side edges smooth and working 3 sc at each point of triangle. Break off A; attach C. Working in both loops of each stitch, work 1 rnd with C, then 2 rnds with B, increasing at corners.

SQUARE BLOCKS: Make 25. Work same as for triangular block until point is made. Break off A. Turn work upside down and attach A to foundation chain. (*Note:* Foundation chain will be at horizontal center of square block.) Work sc in each loop along unworked side of foundation chain (46 sc). Ch 2, turn. Work same as for Row 2 until point is made. Do not break off, but crochet a row of sc around block, working 3 sc at each point. Break off A; crochet 1 rnd with C, the 2 rnds with B.

ASSEMBLY: Following Placement Diagram neatly join square blocks and triangular blocks.

GRAPEVINE: *Note:* The grape clusters, leaves, and vines were worked and positioned with a free hand, rather than in a repetitive pattern. The grapevine shown on one block of the Placement Diagram is simply a suggested placement (directions for grapes and leaf-shapes are given below). Once you are started, feel free to create your own, unique design, making and placing pieces as you desire.

    Stems: With H, crochet chain of desired length.

Grapes: With D, E, F, or G, ch 3. Join with sl st to form ring. **Rnd 1:** Work 12 sc over ring. **Rnd 2:** * Draw up a loop in each of next 2 sc, yo and draw through all loops on hook; repeat from * around. Break off, leaving end. Thread yarn end into tapestry needle, lace through each stitch of Rnd 2, draw sts together and fasten off.

Small leaf: (*Note:* Work in back loop only of each sc.) With H, ch 6. **Row 1:** Sc in 2nd, 3rd, 4th, and 5th ch from hook, sl st in last ch. Ch 1, turn. **Row 2:** Work 2 sc in sl st, sc in next 4 sc. Ch 2, turn. **Row 3:** Skip first 2 sc, sc in next 3 sc, sl st in last sc. Ch 1, turn. **Row 4:** Skip sl st, sc in next 2 sc, 2 sc in last sc. Ch 1, turn. **Row 5:** Sc in first 3 sc, sl st in next sc. Break off.

Medium leaf: (*Note:* Work in back loop only of each sc.) With H, ch 11. **Row 1:** Sc in 2nd ch from hook and in next 8 ch, sl st in last ch. Ch 1, turn. **Row 2:** Sc in sl st, sc in next 7 sc. Ch 1, turn. **Row 3:** Sc in first 7 sc, sl st in last sc. Ch 1, turn. **Row 4:** Sc in sl st, sc in next 4 sc. Ch 1, turn. **Row 5:** Sc in first 4 sc, sl st in next sc; then, working around base of leaf, sc over end st of row 3; then, working into each loop along unworked side of foundation chain, sc in next 8 ch. Break off.

Large Leaf: (*Note:* Work in back loop only of each sc.) With H, ch 3. **Row 1:** Sc in 2nd ch from hook, sl st in last ch. Ch 1, turn. **Row 2:** Work 2 sc in sl st, sc in next sc. Ch 4, turn. **Row 3:** Sc in 2nd, 3rd, and 4th ch from hook, sc in next 2 sc, sl st in last sc. Ch 1, turn. **Row 4:** Work 2 sc in sl st, sc in next 5 sc. Ch 3, turn. **Row 5:** Sc in 2nd and 3rd ch from hook, sc in next 6 sc, sl st in last sc. Ch 1, turn. **Row 6:** Sc in next 9 sts. Ch 1, turn. **Row 7:** Sl st in first 2 sc, sc in next 5 sc, sl st in next sc. Ch 1, turn. **Row 8:** Sc in next 6 sts. Ch 1, turn. **Row 9:** Sl st in first 3 sc, sc in next 2 sc, sl st in next sc. Ch 1, turn. **Row 10:** Skip first st, sc in next 2 sc. Do not break off, but turn work and sc around base of leaf to beginning row. Break off.

Continue to work leaves in this manner, varying shaped edges as desired.

To Attach Grapevine: You may wish to attach clusters of grapes, leaves, and stems block by block, crocheting pieces as you go. On the original afghan, 6 blocks contained a large grape cluster in maroon shades, 9 blocks in blue shades, while the remaining blocks were decorated only around the edge with small clusters of 3 to 6 grapes, leaves, and stems. Lay out pieces in desired arrangement. Sew on vines and leaves, then scatter grapes along the vine, in small groups near leaves or in large clusters with darker shade on one side of cluster and lighter shade on other side.

TASSELS: See Tassels, page 196. With B, make 8 tassels with 20 strands, each 25″ long, tied, folded, and tied again 2″ below top. Trim tassels to 12″. Attach a tassel securely to each point along side edges of afghan.

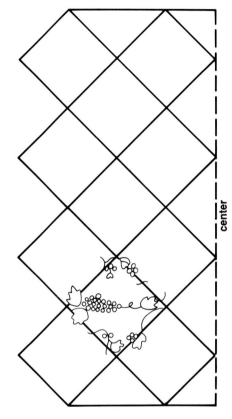

Placement Diagram

"New Bedford, Massachusetts, 50 Years Ago"

Wall hanging or throw, executed in double knit by Judith Gurney of Rochester, Massachusetts

"Any scene can be adapted to graph paper and knitted into a picture afghan," says this designer.

About Judith Gurney

Inspired by an original lithograph of a nineteenth-century painting by William G. Wall, Judith Gurney created this charming and original work. The story of the quaint New England village is pointedly told through her double-knit technique, in which light areas on one side reverse to dark on the other. First, on the front side, the town is bathed in early daylight. The wagon sets out on its morning journey, moving from the right corner to the left. When the hanging is flipped to the back side, the wagon returns home, moving from left to right, in a mysterious, moonlit silence. Describing her knitting as an "obsession," Judith has made many "knitted pictures" for members of her family, always using historical scenes. Judith says, "Local history is my second hobby. My family has lived in southeastern Massachusetts for fourteen generations, beginning with the *Mayflower* Pilgrims."

SIZE: About 47″ × 56″

MATERIALS: Yarn: Knitting worsted, 30 oz each brown (color B) and natural white (W); **knitting needles:** 36″-long circular needle size 10½ (6.50 mm) *or the size that gives you the correct gauge;* **crochet hook (optional):** size I (5.50 mm).

GAUGE: 13 (k 1, p 1) units = 4″; 5 rows = 1″.

Note: Afghan is worked in one piece in double knitting. See Double Knit, page 201, and make practice swatch before beginning afghan.

    Units: *B unit* means k 1 B, yf, p 1 W, yb. *W unit* means k 1 W, yf, p 1 B, yb.

AFGHAN: Starting along side edge (turn book sideways to read chart), with B and W, cast on 308 sts, alternating colors on each st. Do not join sts on circular needle, but work back and forth in rows. **Row 1** (Row 1 on chart): Work W units (see note above) across row. **Row 2** (Row 2 on chart): Work B units across row. **Row 3:** Work W units across row. **Row 4:** Work 2 B units, * 1 W unit, 1 B unit; repeat from * across to last 2 units, work 2 more B units. **Row 5:** Work 2 W units, work B units to last 3 units, work 3 W units. **Row 6:** Work 2 B units, 2 W units, work B units across to last 4 units, work 1 W unit, 3 B units. Continue following Chart 1 from 7th row, reading from right to left on odd-numbered rows and left to right on even-numbered rows, following color key carefully to work reversible design. Mark off rows on chart as you complete them, to help keep your place. Complete Chart 1 through Row 138 (center of afghan), then continue by following Chart 2 from Row 139 through Row 274. Bind off.

FINISHING: Crochet a row of sc around afghan, spacing sts to keep edges smooth and flat and working 3 sc at each corner.

Color Key

even-numbered rows

W unit (k1W, p1B)

B unit (k1B, p1W)

uneven-numbered rows

B unit (k1B, p1W)

W unit (k1W, p1B)

Reverse Side

Each square = one stitch

Chart 1

1   7

138

75

Chart 2

139

224

76

Whales Ahoy!

A good beginner project, a spread crocheted and
cross-stitched by Margaret Hendrickson of La Canade,
California

This was a wedding gift that had to be finished in
two weeks. So the designer chose to make it in
panels, in single crochet, with embroidered motifs.

About Margaret Hendrickson

Whales are a family fascination for the Hendricksons,
stimulated by their youngest daughter's experience
with a whale research team from the Memorial
University of Newfoundland in 1983. More recently,
when two of her daughter's colleagues announced their
engagement, Margaret designed this unique wedding
gift. It was a race against time. First Margaret studied
whales—humpback, sperm, blue, finback, minke—to
capture their markings and proportions with charm as
well as accuracy. With only two weeks then remaining to finish the gift, Margaret didn't have time to
block out a total crochet pattern for a piece this big,
so she decided to cross-stitch the design—a
resourceful solution.

SIZE: About 50″ × 66″, plus 4½″ fringes

MATERIALS: Yarn: Knitting worsted, 45 oz off-white (color A), 6 oz each black (B), charcoal heather (C), medium gray heather (D), medium gray (E), light silver gray (F), small amount of white (G); **crochet hook:** size H (5.00 mm) *or the size that gives you the correct gauge;* large-eyed tapestry needle.

GAUGE: 4 sc = 1″; 4 rows sc = 1″.

Note: Off-white panels are crocheted first, then embroidered. The gray strips are then added and completed pieces are joined.

CENTER PANEL: Starting at one end, with color A, ch 60. **Row 1:** Sc in 2nd ch from hook and in each remaining ch across (59 sc). Ch 1, turn. **Row 2:** Sc in each sc across. Ch 1, turn. Repeat last row until 269 rows have been completed. Break off.

SIDE PANELS: Make 2. With A, ch 25. Work even on 24 sc until 269 rows have been completed. Break off.

EMBROIDERY: For embroidered designs, see charts and work a cross-stitch over each sc (see Cross-Stitch, page 195). *Note:* Along edge of whale shapes, half cross-stitches, rather than full cross-stitches, were sometimes worked to achieve smoother curves. Work only half of stitch, slanting to either the left or right, to conform to the whale's outline.

 Center Panel: Mark 10th row from bottom of center panel. Starting with first row (arrow) of Chart 1 on marked row, embroider design, following color key. Complete chart, then leave 3 sc rows free and start Chart 2 (which is an extension of Chart 1) at arrow. Complete Chart 2. Leave last 6 rows at top of panel unworked.

 Left Side Panel: Mark 9th row from bottom of one side panel. Starting with first row of Chart 3 on marked row, embroider design. Leave 12 rows unworked above design. Now embroider Chart 4 design. Leaving 12 rows unworked between designs, alternate Charts 3 and 4 along left panel (8 whales), leaving 9 rows unworked at top edge.

 Right Side Panel: Work right side panel in same manner as left panel, but leaving only 11 rows unworked between designs and 16 rows unworked at top edge. Embroider your initials or the date on unworked rows at top edge.

Nosy Bears

Crib afghan crocheted by Marsha Horstmann of Norfolk, Virginia

These "nosy" bears don't have colds, but do have stuffed noses. Children will love their three-dimensional look and feel.

About Marsha Horstmann

Marsha Horstmann's three-and-a-half-year-old daughter's collection of stuffed bears inspired this adorable afghan, and delighted the child from the start. "Stephanie enjoyed looking at all the squares as I finished them," says Marsha. She worked each unit separately, using a variation of the granny-square technique she had learned when she was eleven, from her grandmother. The bright backgrounds that frame the little bear faces create a very cheerful coverlet. They also put a great deal of leftover yarn to use.

SIZE: About 38″ × 45″

MATERIALS: Yarn: Knitting worsted, 16 oz white (color W), 3½ oz each brown, tan, gold, and black for bear's faces, small amounts of pink, blue, and other bright colors; **crochet hook:** size F (4.00 mm) *or size that gives you the correct gauge;* tapestry needle; small amount of polyester or cotton batting for stuffing bear snouts.

GAUGE: 9 dc = 2″; 2 rows = 1″. Each block measures about 7½″ square.

BASIC BLOCK: See Blocks, page 85, for colors. **Bear's Face:** starting at center, ch 2. **Rnd 1 (right side):** Work 6 sc in 2nd ch from hook. Do not join, but work around and around with right side facing you. Mark beginning of rnds. **Rnd 2:** Work 2 sc in each sc around (12 sc). **Rnd 3:** * Sc in next sc, 2 sc in next sc; repeat from * around (18 sc). **Rnd 4:** * 2 sc in next sc, sc in next 2 sc; repeat from * around (6 sc inc). Continue in this manner for 4 more rnds, increasing 6 sc each rnd and being careful not to work inc directly over those of previous rnd (48 sc). Sl st in next sc and break off.

Snout: Work same as for face for 4 rnds. **Rnd 5:** Sc in each sc around. **Rnd 6:** * Sc in 3 sc, 2 sc in next sc; repeat from * around (30 sc). **Rnd 7:** Sc in each sc around. Sl st in next sc and break off.

Ears: Make 2. Starting at inner ear with contrasting color, ch 2. **Row 1 (right side):** Work 6 sc in 2nd ch from hook. Ch 1, turn. **Row 2:** Work 2 sc in each sc around, working off last 2 loops of last sc on row with same color as on face to change colors. Break off contrasting color. Ch 1, turn. **Row 3:** With same color as for face, sc in first sc, (2 sc in next sc, sc in next sc) 5 times, sc in last sc. Break off, leaving end for sewing.

Nose: Ch 2. **Rnd 1 (right side):** Work 6 sc in 2nd ch from hook. Sl st in first sc. Break off.

Border: Attach bright-color yarn to any sc on edge of bear's face. **Rnd 1:** Ch 5, * skip next sc, dc in next sc, ch 2; repeat from * around, ending sl st in 3rd ch of ch 5 (24 ch-2 sp, including remaining 2 ch of ch 5). Do not turn. **Rnd 2:** Ch 3, work (2 dc, ch 1, 3 dc) over first ch 2 (first corner made), * work (3 dc over next ch 2) twice, work (3 dc, ch 1, 3 dc) over next ch 2 (corner made); repeat from * 6 times more, work (3 dc over next ch 2) twice, sl st to top of ch 3 (octagon made; edges may not lie completely flat). **Rnd 3:** Ch 1, sc in next dc, skip 1 dc, * work 2 sc over corner ch 1, (skip 1 dc, sc in next dc at center of 3-dc group, skip 1 dc, sc between 3-dc groups) 3 times, skip 1 dc, sc in next dc, skip 1 dc; repeat from * around, ending with sl st in first sc. **Rnd 4:** Sl st in next sc, * ch 16, skip 9 sc on next side of octagon, sl st in 2nd sc on next corner, sl st in next 8 sc, ending in first sc of next corner; repeat from * around, ending with sl st in last 7 sc. Break off colored yarn. Attach W to 9th ch of one ch-16 loop. **Rnd 5:** Ch 3, dc in same ch where yarn was attached, * dc in next 7 ch, dc in back loop of sl sts, dc in 7 ch of next ch-16 loop; for corner work 2 dc in next ch, ch 1, 2 dc in next ch; repeat from * around to last corner, work 2 dc in last ch, ch 1, sl st in top of ch 3 (4 corners); do not turn. **Rnd 6:** Ch 3, work dc in same place as sl st, * dc in next 25 dc, 2 dc in next dc before corner, work 2 dc in corner ch-1 sp, 2 dc in next dc; repeat from * around to last corner, working 2 dc in ch-1 sp, sl st in top of ch 3. Break off.

To complete block: Stuff snout lightly and sew off-center to bear's face (lower edge of snout at bottom edge of face and top of snout covering center of face). Sew nose to center of snout. Embroider eyes above snout with small straight stitches. Spread lower edge of ears to form V; sew V edge in place at top of face.

BLOCKS: Make 30 in all. Following directions for basic block, make bears' heads as follows: make 6 heads with tan face and snout, brown inner ears, and black nose and eyes; 6 heads with gold face and snout, tan, gold, or brown inner ears, black nose and eyes; 6 heads with brown face and snout, pink inner ears, nose, and eyes; 12 heads with black face and nose, white snout and inner ears, blue eyes. Use any bright color for border.

ROSES: Make 20. With W, ch 2. **Rnd 1:** Work 6 sc in 2nd ch from hook. **Rnd 2:** Working in front loop only work (3 dc, sc) in each sc around. **Rnd 3:** Push sts of Rnd 2 forward and, reaching behind these sts, work (3 dc, sc) in back loop of each sc on Rnd 1. Break off.

ASSEMBLY: Lay out blocks in desired color arrangement, having 5 across and 6 down. Sew edges together with yarn, matching sts. Sew a rose at each corner joining where 4 blocks meet.

BORDER: With right side facing you, attach W to one corner of afghan. **Rnd 1:** Sc in each st around, working (sc, ch 1, sc) in 2nd of the 2 dc in corners sl st in first-sc. **Rnd 2:** Ch 3, * work 3 dc in next sc (shell), sc in next sc; repeat from * around, working (5 dc in ch-1 sp, skip next sc) in corners. Sl st in top of ch 3. Break off.

Patchwork Squares

Spread worked in afghan stitch, with cross-stitch embroidery by Susan Lowe of Baton Rouge, Louisiana

Crocheting a quilt is quicker than sewing one, according to the designer of this easy project.

About Susan Lowe

Here is Susan Lowe's humorous description of her first crocheted afghan, attempted eighteen years ago: "It took my entire three years of nursing school to complete. It was a granny square consisting of many different dye lots, and was a mess! My dog later claimed it as his." Sound familiar? Even the most frustrated beginner will be encouraged to see Susan's work today and to learn that she has garnered many first-place ribbons over the years. When Susan and her family moved to Baton Rouge a few years ago, she found quilting very popular there, and she became particularly attracted to the brightly colored lap-quilt patterns. Though an accomplished quilter, Susan says she prefers to crochet her quilts. Her *Woman's Day* afghan is scheduled to hang in the narthex of her church.

SIZE: About 60″ × 79″

MATERIALS: Yarn: Knitting worsted, 52 oz ecru, 48 oz taupe, 4 oz each light blue, bright yellow, red, baby pink, mint green, Kelly green, lilac; 2 oz each medium blue, burgundy, tan, brown, pale yellow, bright pink; **hook:** 14″-long afghan hook size F (4.00 mm) *or the size that gives you the correct gauge;* tapestry needle.

GAUGE: 9 sts = 2″; 9 rows = 2″. Each finished block with border measures about 16″ square.

PATTERN STITCH: Plain Afghan Stitch. See Plain Afghan Stitch, page 195.

BLOCK: Make 12. With ecru, ch 51. Work in plain afghan st on 50 sts for 50 rows. Sl st in each st across. Break off.

BLOCK BORDER: Make 12. With ecru, ch 73. Work in plain afghan st on 72 sts for 10 rows. **Right edge:** Working on first 11 sts only, work 50 more rows. Break off. **Left edge:** Attach ecru to 12th st of 10th row, sl st across center 50 sts; working on last 11 sts only, work 50 more rows, ch 50. Break off. **Top edge:** Attach ecru to first st of upper right edge. Work across 11 sts of right edge, work st in each ch of ch 50, work across 11 sts of left edge. Work on 72 sts for 10 rows more to create a frame. Sl st in each st across. Break off.

JOINING STRIPS: A strips: Make 9. With taupe, ch 73. Work in plain afghan st on 72 sts for 12 rows. Sl st in each st across. Break off. **B strips:** Make 4. With taupe, ch 16. Work in plain afghan st on 15 sts for 316 rows. Sl st in each st across. Break off. **C strips:** Make 2. With taupe, ch 277. Work in plain afghan st on 276 sts for 12 rows. Sl st in each st across. Break off.

EMBROIDERY: See Cross-Stitch over Afghan Stitch, page 195. Following Charts 1 through 12 and Color Key, embroider a different patchwork design on each block, leaving 1 st unworked at each edge. Leaving 1 st along outer edge of border unworked, embroider each block border, following Border Chart and Color Key and turning chart to work each corner.

ASSEMBLY: With ecru yarn, sew a block into center opening of each border. Following Assembly Diagram, join blocks and A strips in 3 vertical units; join B strips to sides of units; join C strips to top and lower edges.

Note: A single block, with block border added, would make a handsome pillow top to match your afghan.

Each square = one stitch

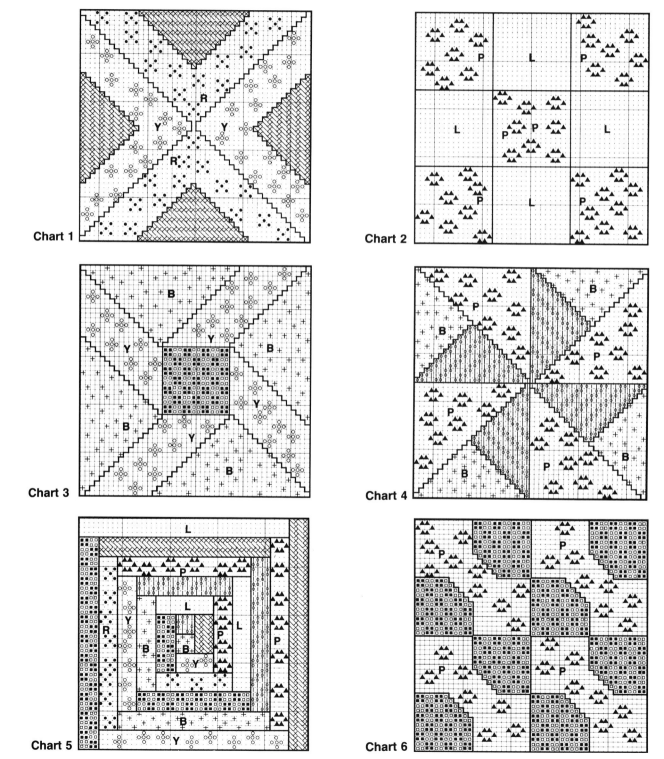

Chart 1

Chart 2

Chart 3

Chart 4

Chart 5

Chart 6

Color Key for Embroidery

- ⊟ = light blue
- ⊞ = medium blue (B)
- ⏀ = bright yellow (Y)
- ⊓ = pale yellow
- ⦿ = burgundy
- ◉ = red (R)
- ◼ = brown
- ⬚ = tan (T)
- △ = baby pink
- ▲ = bright pink
- ⧄ = lilac (L)
- ◺ = mint green
- ⊠ = kelly green
- ☐ = unworked
  background

Each square = one stitch

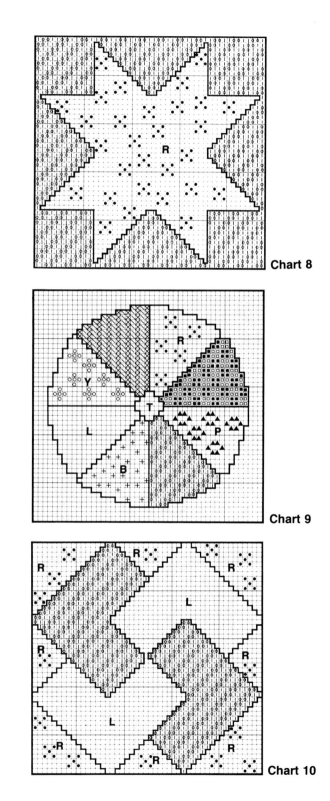

Chart 8

Chart 9

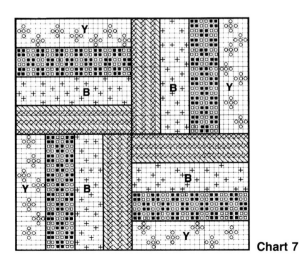

Chart 7

Chart 10

91

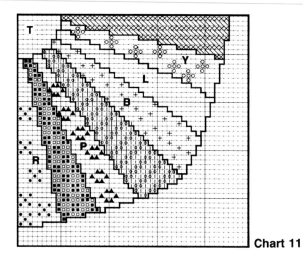

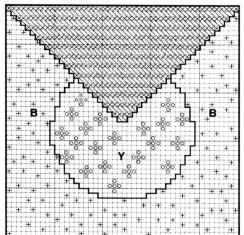

Chart 11

Chart 12

Border Chart

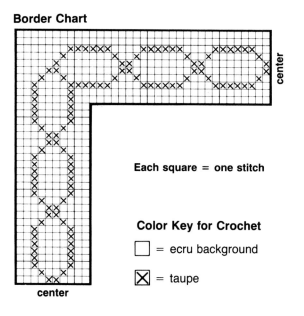

center

center

Each square = one stitch

Color Key for Crochet

☐ = ecru background

☒ = taupe

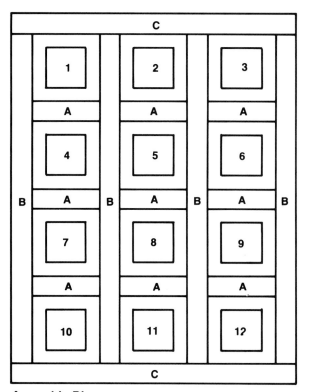

Assembly Diagram

Pastel Patchwork

Pieced coverlet done in single crochet, with cross-stitch joinings, by Patricia McCarty of Williamsport, Pennsylvania

This is a great (and easy) lap project, with squares, rectangles, and triangles worked separately, and then pieced together like an old-fashioned quilt.

About Patricia McCarty

Patricia McCarty, like so many left-handed needle-workers, remembers how difficult it was to learn to crochet from others: "Everything was backwards," says Pat. Well, with perseverance she was able to teach herself, and she has enjoyed a rewarding hobby for the last ten years. Her contest entry is a crisp, fresh interpretation of an old pieced-quilt design. Says Pat, "I love old quilts, so I decided to design a quilt afghan. I chose the colors because they were light and cheerful and blended together beautifully." It took Pat about three and a half weeks to complete her project. "I worked on it while my children were in school," adds this busy mother of three.

SIZE: About 46″ × 65″

MATERIALS: Yarn: Knitting worsted, 24½ oz white (color W), 14 oz mint green (M), 10½ oz each lemon yellow (Y) and light orange (O), 7 oz pink (P), and 3½ oz lavender (L); **crochet hook:** size J (6.00 mm) *or the size that gives you the correct gauge;* large-eyed tapestry needle.

GAUGE: 3 sc = 1″. Each block with its white border measures about 19″ square.

BLOCKS: Make 6. Make each block as follows: **Center Square:** Make 1 for each block. With M, ch 16. **Row 1:** Sc in 2nd ch from hook and in each remaining ch across (15 sc). Ch 1, turn. **Row 2:** Sc in each sc across. Ch 1, turn. Repeat Row 2 until 18 rows are completed. Break off. Block to 5″ square. **Yellow and Orange Squares:** Make 4. With Y, ch 16. Work same as for Center Square until 9 rows are completed. Break off Y; attach O. With O, sc 9 rows. Break off. Block to 5″ square. **Triangles:** Make 4 with P, 4 with M. Starting at point, ch 2. **Row 1:** Sc in 2nd ch from hook. Ch 1, turn. **Row 2:** Work 3 sc in sc. Ch 1, turn. **Row 3:** Work 2 sc in first sc, sc in next sc, 2 sc in last sc (5 sc). Ch 1, turn. **Row 4:** Work 2 sc in first sc, sc to last sc, 2 sc in last sc (2 sc inc). Ch 1, turn. Repeat Row 4 seven times more (21 sc). Break off. Block to form a right triangle with short sides measuring 5″. Sew long edge of M triangle to each P triangle to make four 5″ squares.

    Block Assembly: Following Assembly Diagram, neatly sew squares together with matching yarns for center of block.

    Block Border: Attach W to a corner of block. Work 6 rnds of sc all around block, working 3 sc in st at each corner. Break off.

AFGHAN ASSEMBLY: Sew blocks together to form panel 2 blocks wide and 3 blocks long.

FINISHING: Inner Border: Attach W to a corner of panel. Working in back loop only of each st, sc in each sc around, working 3 sc in st at each corner, for 2 rnds. Working through both loops of each st, sc in each sc around, working 3 sc in st at each corner, for 4 more rnds. Break off.

    Triangle Border: Make 35 triangles each of O and M, 34 of Y. Work same as for block triangles until 7 rows (13 sc) are completed. Break off.

SIZE: About 50″ × 64″

MATERIALS: Yarn: Knitting worsted, 52 oz scrap yarn in assorted bright colors, including about 3½ oz each of colors A, B, and C for borders and last rnd of motifs (designer used navy, medium blue, and dark blue on original afghan); **crochet hook:** size H (5.00 mm) *or the size that gives you the correct gauge.*

GAUGE: Each motif measures 5″ across from curve to curve.

Note: Use any color except A or B for Rnds 1 through 4 of motifs. Work Rnd 5 with A, B, or C. All rnds are worked from right side.

MOTIF: Make 120. Starting at center, ch 4; join with sl st to form ring. **Rnd 1 (right side):** Ch 3 (counts as first dc), dc in ring, work (ch 1, 2 dc in ring) 5 times, ch 1; join with sl st to top of ch 3 (six 2-dc groups made). Fasten off. **Rnd 2:** Join next color in any ch-1 sp, work (ch 3, dc, ch 1, 2 dc) in same sp, * work (2 dc, ch 1, 2 dc) in next ch-1 sp; repeat from * around; join. (*Note:* Next rnd can be worked with same or different color.) **Rnd 3:** Sl st to next ch-1 sp, ch 3, 6 dc in same sp, * skip 4 dc, work 7 dc in next ch-1 sp; repeat from * around; join. Fasten off. **Rnd 4:** Join next color in first dc of any group, sc in same dc and in next 6 dc, * make long sc around Rnds 2 and 3 in next sp between dc groups on Rnd 2, sc in next 7 dc; repeat from * around, ending with long sc; join. Fasten off. **Rnd 5:** Join A, B, or C in any sc; sc in each sc around; join. Fasten off.

FINISHING: Sewing through back loops of 2 or 3 corresponding sc on top of 2 curves, join motifs in 10 strips of 12 motifs each using matching yarn. Sew strips together, side by side, as shown in Joining Diagram. Upper and lower edges have large spaces to be filled in; sides remain saw-toothed.

    Fill-in Spaces on Upper and Lower Edges: Row 1: With right side of afghan facing you, using A or B, join yarn to first sc on center motif in space (X on Joining Diagram); ch 3, skip about ½″ on side of space and sl st in sc (W); rotate work and dc in each sc across center motif, work 2 dc in last sc, sl st in side edge (Y). **Row 2:** Ch 3, skip ½″ on side edge, sl st in edge (Z); turn work, dc in

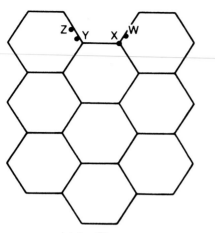

Joining Diagram

front loop of each dc across, work 2 dc in last st, sl st in side edge. (*Note:* Inc at sides as needed to keep work flat.) **Row 3:** Work as for Row 2, working in back loop of each dc. Fasten off, or work a 4th row of dc if necessary to make straighter edge. Fill in corners of afghan in same manner, working ch 3 and turn on outer edges. **Border: Rnds 1 and 2:** From right side, working with A or B, sc in back loop of each st around afghan. Fasten off. **Scalloped Edging:** with right side facing you, work across one end as follows: join A or B in corner, * sc in 2 sc, skip 1 sc, work 7 dc in next sc, skip 1 sc; repeat from * across, ending with 2 sc, sl st. Fasten off. Repeat edging across opposite end to complete afghan.

Aztec/Mayan Mystique

Spectacular spread crocheted in afghan stitch and
embroidered in cross-stitch by Felicia Nelson
of Kankakee, Illinois

Truly a work of art, the original was worked in a single
piece, with center and side panels embroidered in
cross-stitch and outlined in backstitch. Our instructions
enable you to work the afghan in three panels.

About Felicia Nelson

For almost thirty years the Nelsons have lived along
the banks of the Kankakee, where, says Felicia, "we
experienced the joys and sorrows of life on an unpre-
dictable river." This may partially explain Felicia's affin-
ity with the ancient symbols of the Indians of the
Americas that show up in her afghan, such as the stair-
step motif with which Indians so often suggest mountains and rivers. To avoid boring repetition, she varied
the medallions' colors and shapes. Then, combining
contemporary with ancient, Felicia introduced into her
border a stylized modern-day table telephone, along
with the arrow, a traditional Native American symbol
of communication and friendship.

SIZE: About 78″ wide × 68″, plus 5″ fringe

MATERIALS: Yarn: Knitting worsted, 80 oz white (color W), 14 oz black (BK), 10 oz red (R), 7 oz each gold (GO), orange (O), and yellow (Y), 3 oz each medium brown (MB), dark brown (DB), medium blue (B), navy (N), aqua (A), mint green (M), medium green (G), forest green (FG), salmon (S), pale yellow (PY), and lilac (L); **hooks:** 14″-long aluminum afghan hooks sizes I (5.50 mm) and J (6.00 mm) *or sizes that give you the correct gauge;* tapestry needle.

GAUGE: With larger hook, 7 sts = 2″; 3 rows = 1″.

PATTERN STITCH: Plain Afghan Stitch. See Plain Afghan Stitch page 195.

CENTER PANEL: *Note:* Original afghan was worked as a single large center panel and a border panel along each side edge. Because of the large number of stitches required for the center panel, you may find it easier to work the panel in 3 pieces; directions are given for both methods.

    Single-Panel Center: With W and larger hook, loosely ch 235. Work in plain afghan stitch on 234 sts. Push sts together tightly to fit onto hook as you work across each row. To avoid unraveling, be sure to complete a whole row, working off all loops, before laying work down when you wish to stop. When 204 rows are completed, sl st in each st across last row. Break off.

    3-Panel Center: Make 3 panels. With W and larger hook, loosely ch 79. Work in plain afghan stitch on 78 sts for 204 rows. Sl st in each st across. Break off. Matching rows, with W neatly sew panels together along side edges to form panel of 234 sts across and 204 rows in length.

BORDER: Make 2. With R and smaller hook, ch 24. (*Note:* More rows–219–are worked on border panels than on center panel. Work to slightly tighter gauge on smaller hook so all panels are same length when completed.) Work in plain afghan stitch on 23 sts for 22 rows, then work rows and colors as follows: 22 rows with PY, 8 L, 5 G, 9 L, 18 MB, 22 GO, 20 S, 18 O, 9 A, 5 DB, 8 A, 19 S, 34 GO. Sl st in each st across. Break off.

ASSEMBLY: Sew borders to sides of center panel, easing to fit smoothly.

Color Key

- ■ or BK = black
- ● or DB = dark brown
- ⊞ or MB = medium brown
- ☐ or W = white
- ⊡ or B = medium blue
- ▲ or N = navy
- ◺ or A = aqua
- ⊟ or G = medium green
- ◣ or FG = forest green
- ⋁ or M = mint green
- ⊠ or R = red
- △ or S = salmon
- ◿ or GO = gold
- ⊠ or Y = yellow
- ⎔ or PY = pale yellow
- ◺ or O = orange
- ▭ or L = lilac

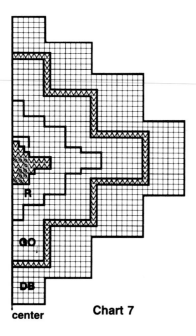

center **Chart 7**

Motif 22: With N, backstitch around each O area.

Motif 23: With R, backstitch around inner B area.

Border Panels: Embroider panels following Border Chart. All cross-stitches are worked with BK, except for DB and G area, which are worked in W. Undesignated areas on chart are unworked background. Arrow shafts, shown as broken lines, are worked in backstitch with a diagonal st (half a cross-stitch) worked over every other backstitch. Work arrow feathers with straight stitches as indicated.

FINISHING: With W, crochet a row of sc across top and bottom edges of afghan. **Fringes:** See Fringes, page 196. Using yarn remaining from embroidery and mixing colors in each fringe, cut ten 11″ strands of yarn for each fringe. Make a fringe every 2″ all around edge of afghan.

Note: A single motif, embroidered on a square of afghan stitches, would make a handsome pillow top to match your afghan.

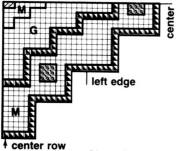

center row **Chart 8**

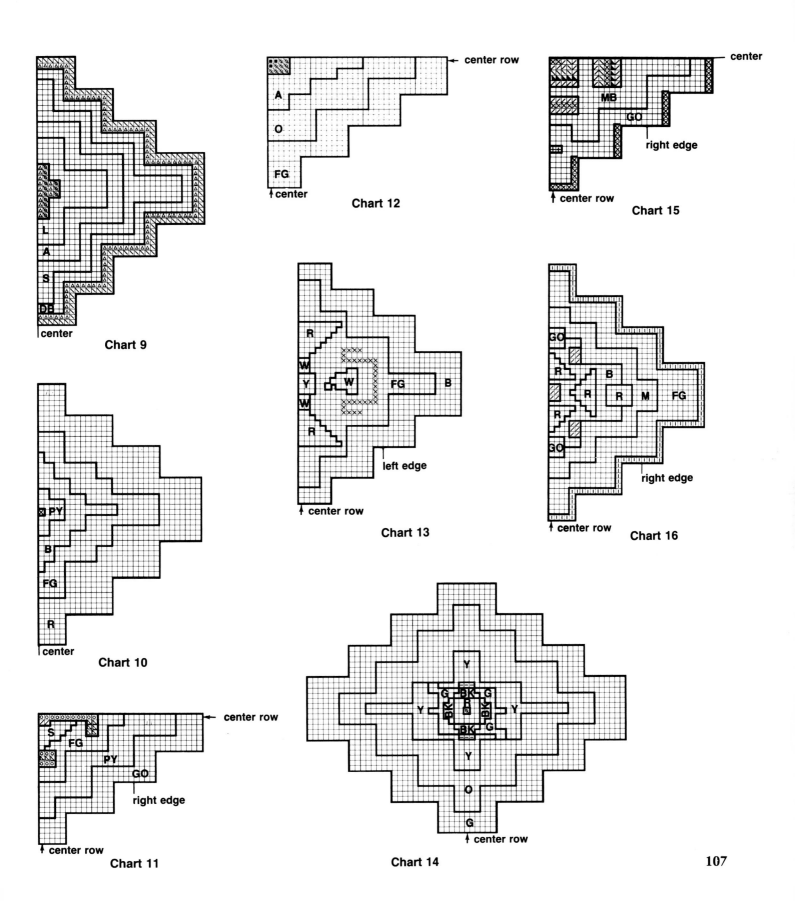

Chart 9

Chart 10

Chart 11

Chart 12

Chart 13

Chart 14

Chart 15

Chart 16

107

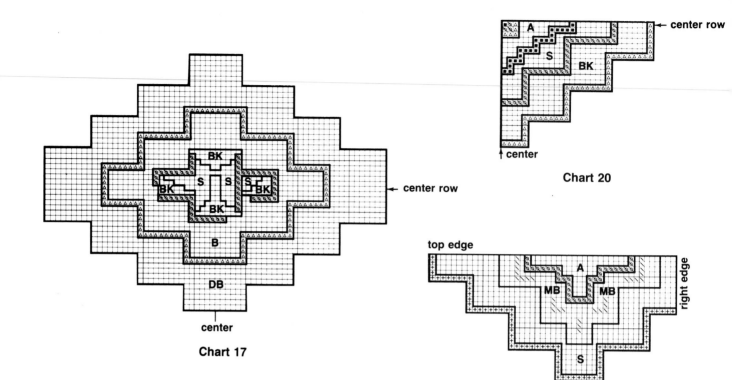

Chart 17

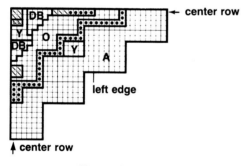

Chart 18

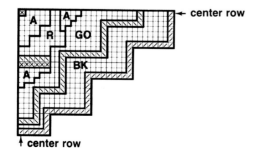

Chart 19

Chart 20

Chart 21

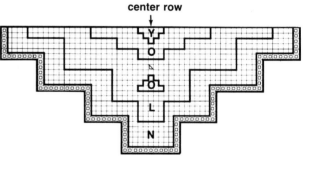

Chart 22

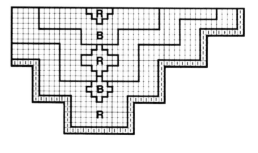

Chart 23

108

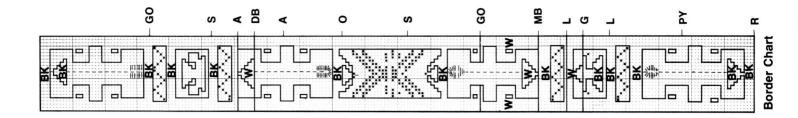

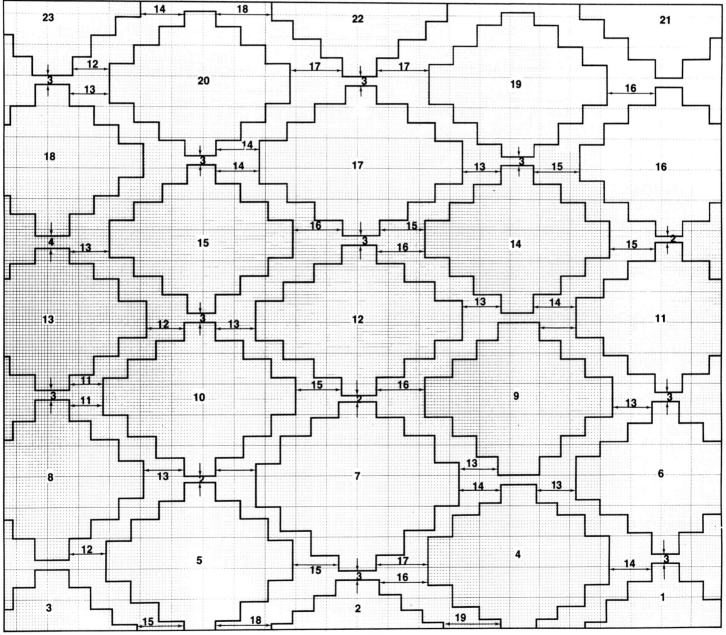

Placement Diagram

Baby Blocks

Crib coverlet crocheted by Sandra Oidtman
of Henley, Missouri

Soft and playful, these pastel blocks will keep
a newborn cosy.

About Sandra Oidtman

Sandra Oidtman explains that although she loves rainbows, whenever she'd think of babies, she'd picture alphabet blocks. So as she planned this afghan for her first grandchild, "I tried to come up with a design based on both my favorites." The six pastel colors suggest the rainbow and, Sandy adds, "I felt the purity of white was a good base color for a baby afghan." Henley is a farm community, says Sandy, located about fifteen miles south of the state capital of Jefferson City, where she works for the Missouri State Data Center. Her family's two-acre lot offers plenty of room for what she describes as a "good-sized garden." In addition to gardening, Sandy's hobbies ("loves of life," as she calls them) include crocheting, sewing, reading, writing, and a new interest in knitting.

SIZE: About 35″ × 41″

MATERIALS: Yarn: Knitting worsted, 8 oz white (MC), 4 oz each pink (A), aqua (B), lavender (C), yellow (D), light blue (E), and peach (F); **crochet hook:** size H (5.00 mm) *or size that gives you the correct gauge.*

GAUGE: Each rectangle = 3″ × 6″; each square = 3″ square.

RECTANGLES: Make 12 (2 each with A, B, C, D, E, and F). Starting at center with colored yarn, ch 12 for foundation. **Row 1:** Work (2 dc, ch 2 for corner loop, 3 dc) in 4th ch from hook, (ch 1, skip 1 ch, 3 dc in next ch) 4 times, ch 2 (corner), 3 dc in last ch (same ch where last 3 dc was worked), ch 2 (corner); working along on other side of foundation, 3 dc in first ch (same ch where last 3 dc was worked), work (ch 1, skip 1 ch, 3 dc in next ch) 4 times, ch 2 (corner); sl st to top of ch 3. **Row 2:** Sl st in next 2 dc and in corner sp, ch 3, in same sp work (2 dc, ch 2, 3 dc), (ch 1, 3 dc in next ch-1 sp between 3-dc groups) 4 times,* ch 1, in next corner sp work (3 dc, ch 2, 3 dc); repeat from * once, (ch 1, 3 dc in next ch-1 sp) 4 times, ch 1, work corner as before in next corner sp, ch 1; sl st in top of ch 3. Break off. **Row 3:** Attach MC in first corner sp, ch 3, work (2 dc, ch 2, 3 dc) in same sp, (ch 1, 3 dc in next space) 5 times, ch 1, in next sp work corner of (3 dc, ch 2, 3 dc), ch 1, 3 dc in next sp, work corner as before in next sp, (ch 1, 3 dc in next sp) 5 times, ch 1, work corner in next sp, ch 1, 3 dc in next sp, ch 1; sl st in top of ch 3. Break off.

Sew blocks together with MC, joining ends of rectangles to form 4 strips of 3 rectangles each. Then join long edges of strips together to form center panel, alternating colors.

CENTER PANEL BORDER: Join MC to one corner of center panel. **Row 1:** Ch 3, work 4 dc (for first shell), ch 2, and 5 dc (for 2nd shell) over corner ch 2; * sc in next sp along panel edge, work 7 dc in next sp (another shell); repeat from * around, working (5 dc, ch 2, 5 dc) at each corner. Sl st in top of ch 3. Break off. **Row 2:** Attach A to corner sp, work (3 sc, ch 2, 3 sc) in same sp, sc in center dc of corner shell, * work 7-dc shell in next sc, sc in center dc of next shell; repeat from * around, working (3 sc, ch 2, 3 sc) at each corner. Join to first sc. Break off. **Row 3:** Attach B to corner sp, ch 3, (work 2 dc, ch 2, 3 dc) in same corner, sc in center sc of corner 3-sc group, skip last sc of 3-sc group, * work 7-dc shell in next sc, sc in center st of next shell; repeat from * around, working (3 dc, ch 2, 3 dc) at each corner. Join to ch 3. Break off. **Row 4:** Attach C to corner sp, work (3 sc, ch 2, 3 sc) in same corner, * work 7-dc shell in next sc, sc in center dc of next shell; repeat from * around, working (3 sc, ch 2, 3 sc) in each corner. Join. Break off. **Row 5:** Attach D to corner sp, ch 3, work (6 dc, ch 2, 7 dc) in same corner, * sc in center dc of next 7-dc shell, work 7-dc shell in next sc; repeat from * around, working (7 dc, ch 2, 7 dc) in each corner. Join. Break off. **Row 6:** With E, repeat Row 2. Break off. **Row 7:** Attach F to corner sp, work (3 sc, ch 2, 3 sc) in same corner, skip last sc of 3-sc group, * work 7-dc shell in next sc, sc in center dc of next shell; repeat from * around, working (3 sc, ch 2, 3 sc) in each corner. Join. Break off. **Row 8:** With MC, repeat Row 5. Break off. Piece should measure about 21″ × 27″.

SQUARES: Make 36 (7 each of B and D, 6 each of A, C, and E, 4 of F). Starting at center with colored yarn, ch 4. Join with sl st to form ring. **Rnd 1:** Ch 3, work 2 dc in ring, (ch 2, 3 dc in ring) 3 times, ch 2; join to top of ch 3. **Rnd 2:** Sl st in next 2 dc and in ch-2 sp, ch 3, work first corner of (2 dc, ch 2, 3 dc) in same sp, * ch 1, work corner of (3 dc, ch 2, 3 dc) in next sp; repeat from * twice more, ch 1; join to ch 3. Break off. **Rnd 3:** Attach MC to one corner sp, ch 3, work first corner of (2 dc, ch 2, 3 dc) in same sp, (ch 1, 3 dc in next sp, ch 1, work corner in next sp) 3 times, ch 1, 3 dc in next sp, ch 1; join. Break off.

Alternating colors, sew blocks together to form frame for center panel 9 squares wide and 11 squares long. Join inner edge of frame to edge of center panel as follows: with right side facing you, attach MC to corner of panel. Sl st in corner st; then hold corner of frame behind panel, wrong sides touching, and sl st in next st, working st through both panel and frame; then, working through panel layer only, sl st in each edge st of panel to center of next shell and sl st in next st through both layers of panel and frame, catching edge of frame at corresponding point of frame edge to keep edges smooth and unrippled. Check to be sure right side of work for both panel and frame faces in same direction when pieces lie flat. Continue in this manner, working sl sts on panel edge only to center of each shell, then working a sl st through both layers at each shell center and at each corner of panel.

OUTER BORDER: Attach MC to a corner sp of framed center panel. **Row 1:** Ch 3, work (2 dc, ch 2, 3 dc) in same sp, * work ** (ch 1, 3 dc in next sp) twice, ch 1, work 3 dc in next corner joining of squares; repeat from ** to last square, work (ch 1, 3 dc in next sp) twice, ch 1, work (3 dc, ch 2, 3 dc) in corner sp; repeat from * around, ending with ch 1; join to ch 3. Break off. **Row 2:** Attach F to corner sp, ch 3, (work 2 dc, ch 2, 3 dc) in same sp, * work (ch 1, 3 dc in next sp) across edge to next corner, ch 1, work (3 dc, ch 2, 3 dc) at corner; repeat from * around, ending with ch 1; join to ch 3. Break off. Repeat Row 2 five times working 1 row each with E, D, C, B, and A. **Row 8:** Attach MC to corner sp, ch 3, work (6 dc, ch 2, 7 dc) in same sp, * sc in next sp, work 7-dc shell in next sp; repeat from * around, working (7 dc, ch 2, 7 dc) at each corner. Break off. **Row 9:** With F, sl st in back loop only of each st around. Break off.

Reversible Rainbow

Knitted throw, designed for relatively easy execution, by Ruth Ramminger of Binghamton, New York

Two-color slip-stitch bands alternate with strips of solid-color seed stitch to produce this contemporary afghan which is also reversible.

About Ruth Ramminger

In spite of the demands of homemaking and mothering six children, Ruth Ramminger maintains a high profile as a local artist and craftsperson. Her pastime is knitting, something Ruth says she can pursue "while waiting for car pools, attending baseball games, watching TV, and on long car trips." The slip-stitch technique she uses in this colorful afghan is a handy one to know if you're as busy as Ruth, since it permits a variety of multicolored patterns and textures without the hassles of bobbins and tedious seaming. With enough bright leftover yarns to create a rainbow, Ruth was able to complete her project in three weeks.

SIZE: About 62" (plus 2½" fringes) × 41"

MATERIALS Yarn: Knitting worsted, 6 oz each purple (color A) and magenta (B), 4 oz each red (C), red orange (D), golden orange (E), bright yellow (F), lime green (G), Kelly green (H), turquoise (I), and royal blue (J); **knitting needles:** 36"-long circular needle size 10½ (6.50 mm) *or the size that gives you the correct gauge;* **crochet hook:** size H (5.00 mm).

GAUGE: In ribbing, 5 sts = 1"; 5 rows = 1".

AFGHAN: Starting at long edge using color A, cast on 322 sts. **Border: Row 1:** K across. **Row 2:** K 1, * k 1, with yarn at back of work sl 1 as if to p; repeat from * across to last st, k last st. Repeat last row 7 times more. Drop A; attach B. **Rainbow Stripes: Row 1:** With B, * k 1, yarn forward, sl 1, yarn back, (k 1, p 1) 3 times; repeat from * across to last 2 sts, k 1, yarn forward, sl 1. **Row 2:** With B, * yarn back, sl 1, yarn forward, (p 1, k 1) 3 times, p 1; repeat from * across to last 2 sts, yarn back, sl 1, yarn forward, p 1. **Row 3:** With A, (k 1, p 1) twice, k 1, * yarn forward, sl 1, yarn back, k 1, (p 1, k 1) 3 times; repeat from * to last 5 sts, yarn forward, sl 1, yarn back, (k 1, p 1) twice. **Row 4:** With A, (k 1, p 1) twice, * yarn back, sl 1, yarn forward, p 1, (k 1, p 1) 3 times; repeat from * across to last 6 sts, yarn back, sl 1, yarn forward, (p 1, k 1) twice, p 1. **Rows 5 through 12:** Repeat Rows 1 through 4 of stripes twice more. **Rows 13 and 14:** Repeat Rows 1 and 2 once more. **Rows 15 and 16:** With A, work in k 1, p 1 ribbing. Break off A. **Row 17 (seed st):** With B only, * p 1, k 1; repeat from * across. **Row 18 (seed st):** * K 1, p 1; repeat from * across. **Rows 19 and 20:** Repeat Rows 17 and 18. **Rows 21 and 22:** Work in k 1, p 1 ribbing. **Row 23:** With C, repeat Row 2 of rainbow stripes. **Row 24:** With C, repeat Row 1. **Row 25:** With B, repeat Row 4. **Row 26:** With B, repeat Row 3. **Rows 27 through 34:** Repeat Rows 23 and 24 once more. **Rows 37 and 38:** With B only, work in k 1, p 1 ribbing. Break off B. **Rows 39 through 44:** With C only, repeat Rows 17 through 22. Attach D. Using D in place of B, and C in place of A, repeat Rows 1 through 22. Attach E and with D and E continue in pattern stitch, repeating Rows 23 through 44. Repeat Rows 1 through 44 throughout, breaking off completed colors and adding new colors as follows: F, G, H, I, J, and A, ending with Row 22 of pattern. Break off A. With B only, repeat Row 2 of border 8 times. Bind off.

FINISHING: With B, crochet a row of sl st across cast-on and bound-off edges.

FRINGES: Fringes, page 196. Matching fringes to color of rainbow stripes at side edges, cut three 6″ strands for each fringe. Attach fringes along side edges, spaced about ½″ apart. Trim ends evenly to 2½″.

Wreaths of Rosebuds

Accent piece in afghan stitch and cross-stitch by
Sandie Rice of Cincinnatti, Ohio

Three panels of delicate rosebuds surrounded by cross-
stitched rosettes make a romantic throw.

About Sandie Rice

Sandie Rice is a middle-of-the-night crocheter. Ever
since she developed asthma fifteen years ago, when
she was thirty-one, Sandie has used needlework as a
distraction from not being able to breathe. In recent
years she has done a lot of designing—"my own
sweaters, blankets, and personal items for people."
Before that, until her children were teenagers, she did
nothing but squares. With four children, four
grandchildren, and a set of twin grandchildren on the
way, Sandie decided it was time to redo her living
room, and designed her rosebud afghan to match the
decor of the new room.

SIZE: About 49″ × 52″

MATERIALS: Yarns: Knitting worsted, 60 oz natural; Coats and Clark Luster Sheen, 3 (2-oz—56.7 gr) skeins peach No. 246; 6-strand embroidery floss, 8 skeins light green; **hooks:** 14″-long afghan hook size H (5.00 mm) *or size that gives you the correct gauge,* steel crochet hook size 00; tapestry needle; crepe fabric for lining (optional).

GAUGE: 4 sts = 1″; 4 rows = 1 ″.

PATTERN STITCH: Plain Afghan Stitch. See Plain Afghan Stitch, page 195.

CENTER PANEL: With knitting worsted and afghan hook, ch 67. Work in plain afghan stitch on 66 sts for 201 rows. Sl st in each st across. Break off.

SIDE PANELS: Make 2. With knitting worsted and afghan hook, ch 50. Work in plain afghan stitch on 49 sts for 201 rows. Sl st in each st across. Break off.

EMBROIDERY: See Cross-Stitch over Afghan Stitch, page 195. Also see Embroidery Stitches, page 202. Use 4 strands of green floss for cross-stitches, 6 strands for French knots, and single strand of peach Luster Sheen for satin stitches.

Center Panel: Begin on 2nd row from bottom of panel and 4th st in from right edge. * Following Chart 1 for design, work from W to Y once, repeat from X to Y 8 times, work from Y to Z once, leaving 2 sts unworked at left edge of panel. Repeat from A to B in length 3 times, then from B to C once. Leave next row unworked. Starting on 4th st of next row, follow Chart 2 for design, repeating from W to Y 15 times, then from Y to Z once. When the 2 rows of chart are completed, leave next row unworked. Repeat from * once more. Following Chart 1 for design, work across row as before, working from A to C once. Mark 34th st of next row for center of design. Starting on marked row, embroider Chart 3 design on 28 rows. Embroider flowers with peach satin stitches as indicated. When chart is completed, leave next row unworked. Following Chart 1 for design, work across row as before, working from A to C once. ** Leave next row unworked. Work Chart 2 design on next 2 rows as before. Leave next row unworked. Following Chart 1 for design, work across row as before, repeating from A to B in length 3 times, then from B to C once. Repeat from ** once more, leaving last row unworked at top of panel.

Color Key and Stitch Guide

- ☒ peach cross-stitch
- ☒ green cross-stitch
- ⊙ green French knot

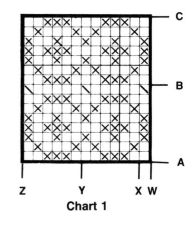

Chart 1

Z Y X W

Chart 2

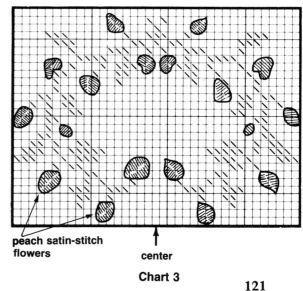

peach satin-stitch flowers

center

Chart 3

121

Side Panels: Begin on 2nd row from bottom of one panel and 4th st in from right edge. * Following Chart 1, work from W to Y once, repeat from X to Y 5 times, work from Y to Z once, leaving 3 sts unworked at left edge of panel. Repeat from A to B in length 3 times, then from B to C once. Leave 1 row unworked. Starting on 4th st of next row, follow Chart 2, repeating from W to Y 10 times, then from X to Z once. When the 2 rows of chart are completed, leave next row unworked. Repeat from * once more. Following Chart 1, work across row as before, working A to C once. Mark 25th st on next row for center of design. Starting with marked row, embroider Chart 3 design on 28 rows. Leave 1 row unworked. Following Chart 1, work across row as before, working form A to C once. ** Leave 1 row unworked. Work Chart 2 design on next 2 rows as before. Leave 1 row unworked. Following Chart 1, work across row as before, repeating from A to B 3 times, then from B to C once. Repeat from ** once more, leaving top row unworked. Repeat for other side panel.

PANEL BORDER: Attach knitting worsted to any st on one side of a panel. With right side of work facing you and using afghan hook, crochet a row of sc around panel, working 3 sc at each corner. **Next row:** Ch 2, work first cluster st as follows: (yo and draw up a loop at base of ch 2) 3 times, yo and draw through all loops on hook, ch 1 to fasten (first cluster st made), * skip 1 sc, make cluster st in next sc as follows: in next sc (yo and draw up a loop) 3 times, yo and draw through all loops on hook, ch 1 to fasten (another cluster st made); repeat from * around, working (cluster st, ch 2 cluster st) at each corner (you may have to adjust number of skipped sts to work corner). End with sl st in first cluster st. Break off. Work panel border around each panel.

ASSEMBLY: Join a side panel to each side edge of center panel by crocheting edges together with sl st worked on wrong side.

FINISHING: Ruffle: Attach peach yarn to a corner. With crochet hook, ch 1, in sp between first 2 cluster sts work (sc, ch 3, sc, ch 3, sc), * in next sp between 2 cluster sts work (sc, ch 3, sc, ch 3, sc); repeat from * around afghan. Break off.

If lining is desired, cut fabric to fit back of each panel. Turn under raw edges and slip-stitch neatly in place.

Lacy Flower Granny

Crocheted coverlet, a good portable project,
by Charlotte Robbins of Westport, Indiana

Individual "flower bursts" create a bright, bold design.

About Charlotte Robbins

"The design of this afghan came about quite by
accident," recalls Charlotte Robbins. It started with one
small crocheted hexagon that grew into a full-blown
tricolored flower. At first Charlotte thought she'd make
pillow covers, but as she kept producing hexagons, she
decided the variegated flowers would produce a
handsome afghan. The piece actually took three
winters to complete: the first to work the hexagons, the
second to attach them, and the third to finish the trim.
A self-taught crocheter, Charlotte says she finds the
craft "very relaxing and rewarding."

SIZE: About 62″ × 82″

MATERIALS: Yarn: Knitting worsted, 42 oz assorted colors, 35 oz off-white (MC); **crochet hook:** size G (4.50 mm) *or the size that gives you the correct gauge.*

GAUGE: Each small hexagon measures about 2¼″ across from point to point.

Note: Each large hexagon is made up of 18 small ones worked in 2 rnds around a center one (see Motif Diagram). Use a different color (but not MC) for center and for each ring; use MC only for assembling and for outer border.

LARGE HEXAGON MOTIF: Make 32. **Small Basic Hexagon (center B on Motif Diagram):** With any color, ch 6; join with sl st to form ring. **Rnd 1:** Ch 5, (dc in ring, ch 2) 5 times; join with sl st in 3rd ch of ch 5 (6 sp made). **Rnd 2:** Work (2 sc, ch 3, 2 sc) in each sp around; join in first sc. Fasten off.

First Ring (R1 hexagons on diagram): With new color, make 6 hexagons around Basic Hexagon as follows: **First Hexagon:** work as for Basic Hexagon through Rnd 1. **Rnd 2 (joining rnd):** Work 2 sc in next sp, ch 1, pick up previous hexagon; holding the two pieces with wrong sides together, sl st in any ch-3 sp on Basic Hexagon, ch 1, 2 sc in same sp on new piece (joining made); work 2 sc in next sp on new piece; ch 1, sl st in next ch-3 sp on Basic Hexagon, ch 1; on new piece work 2 sc in same sp, * 2 sc in next sp, ch 3, 2 sc in same sp; repeat from * around, marking first ch 3 worked; join rnd; fasten off. **Second Hexagon:** Work as for Basic Hexagon through Rnd 1. **Rnd 2 (joining rnd):** Working sc and joinings in sp as for previous hexagon, join to marked loop on previous motif, then to next place where previous 2 motifs are joined, then in next free ch-3 loop on Basic Hexagon; complete rnd from * of Rnd 2 as before on new piece, marking first ch 3. Make and join 4 more hexagons to center in same manner, working extra joining to link first and last hexagons to complete ring.

Second Ring (R2 hexagons on diagram): With new color, work as for first ring, making and joining 12 hexagons to first ring.

SIDE MOTIFS: Make 14. Each Side Motif (enclosed in broken lines on Motif Diagram) is composed of 8 full hexagons and 3 half hexagons.

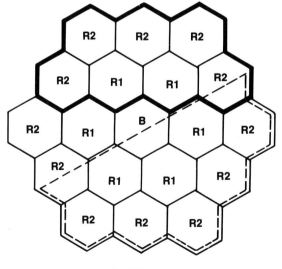

Motif Diagram

125

Color Key

uneven-numbered rows

☒ MC unit (k1MC, p1CC)

☐ CC unit (k1CC, p1MC)

even-numbered rows

☒ CC unit (k1CC, p1MC)

☐ MC unit (k1MC, p1CC)

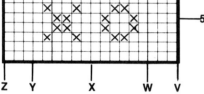

reverse side

SIZE: About 60″ × 45″

MATERIALS: Yarn: Knitting worsted, 28 oz black (MC), 4 oz each of following contrasting colors (CC): red, orange, yellow, green, blue, and purple; **knitting needles:** 36″-long circular needle size 11 (8.00 mm) *or the size that gives you the correct gauge;* **crochet hook:** size J (6.00 mm).

GAUGE: 5 (k 1, p 1) units = 2″; 4 rows = 1″.

Note: Afghan is worked in one piece in double knitting. See Double Knit, page 201, and make a practice swatch before beginning afghan. **Units:** *MC unit* means k 1 MC, yf, p 1 CC, yb. *CC unit* means k 1 CC, yf, p 1 MC, yb.

AFGHAN: Starting at one long edge, with two strands of MC, cast on 300 sts. Drop one strand MC; attach red (CC). **Red Stripe: Row 1** (Row 1 on chart): Work CC units (see Note above) across row. **Row 2:** Work MC units across. **Row 3:** Work 2 units CC, (2 units MC, 3 units CC, 1 unit MC, 2 units CC, 1 unit MC, 3 units CC) 12 times, 2 units MC, 2 units CC. **Row 4:** Work 1 unit CC, (1 unit MC, 2 units CC, 1 unit MC, 3 units CC, 2 units MC, 3 units CC) 12 times, 1 unit MC, 2 units CC, 1 unit MC, 1 unit CC. Now continue following chart from 5th row, and reading chart from W to Y 12 times, then W to X once, following Color Key carefully to work reversible design. When chart is completed, break off CC; pick up MC. Continuing to work double-knit technique with 2 strands MC, work 2 rows. Drop one strand MC; attach orange. **Orange Stripe:** With orange as CC, follow chart, reading from V to W once, W to Y 12 times, then Y to Z once. When chart is completed, break off CC, pick up MC. Double knit 2 rows MC. Drop one strand MC; attach yellow. **Yellow Stripe:** With yellow as CC, follow chart from first row, reading as for red stripe. When chart is completed, break off CC; pick up MC. Double knit 2 rows MC. Drop one strand MC; attach green. **Green Stripe:** With green as CC, follow chart as for orange stripe. Double knit 2 rows MC. **Blue Stripe:** With blue as CC, follow chart from first row as for red stripe. Double knit 2 rows MC. **Purple Stripe:** With purple as CC, follow chart as for orange stripe. Double knit 2 rows MC. Repeat stripe sequence twice more, until 3rd purple stripe is completed. Break off purple. With 2 strands MC, bind off.

FINISHING: With 2 strands MC, crochet row of sc around afghan, spacing sts to keep edges smooth and flat, and working 3 sc at each corner. Weave in any yarn ends so they are hidden between layers.

Child's World

Crocheted coverlet with crocheted appliqués and embroidery by Linda McGregor Scott of Collierville, Tennessee

Create a personalized afghan for your child. Simply apply lettering and small crochet elements to a basic house shape to create scenes from your child's life.

About Linda McGregor Scott

Linda McGregor Scott credits her own childhood memories as the inspiration for this afghan. She recalls the beautiful patchwork in her grandmother's house and the happy hours she spent "driving" toy cars over the designs, which in her imagination "became houses and roads." Using this idea as a departure point, Linda developed an entire "child's world" for her three-year-old son, Aaron. She incorporated scenes familiar to all children—the zoo, the firehouse, etc.—but also personalized her story afghan with a block like the "Florida house with palm trees" where Aaron once lived. Linda loves crafts, she says. But "in defining who I am, the thing I'm most proud of is my role as feature writer and cofounder of our local newspaper, the *Collierville Independent*, created as an alternate to the then only newspaper in town."

● or BK = black

◪ or GO = gold

⊞ or R = red

⊠ or O = orange

◺ or Y = yellow

B = brown

LB = light blue

RB = royal blue

LG = light green

FG = forest green

G = gray

TA = tan

T = turquoise

V = violet

W = white

P = pink

LB

W

FG

h

B

d

FG   FG

p

Each square = one stitch

Basic Block

Z   Y

—1

132

SIZE: About 68″ × 73″

MATERIALS: Yarn: Knitting worsted, 50 oz white (color W), 30 oz light blue (LB), 20 oz forest green (FG), 4 oz black (BK); about 25 oz assorted colors, including pink (P), gold (GO), red (R), orange (O), yellow (Y), brown (B), gray (G), light green (LG), tan (TA), royal blue (RB), violet (V), and turquoise (T). **crochet hook:** size G (4. 50 mm) *or size that gives you the correct gauge;* tapestry needle.

GAUGE: 4 sc = 1″; 9 rows = 2″. Each block measures about 10″ high × 11″ wide.

Note: Afghan is worked in 25 blocks. Charts are given for each of the 10 blocks with special embroidered and appliquéd details. A Basic Chart is provided for the remaining blocks; work house, door, and path in colors of your choice. Vary the basic design, if you like, by working the chart in reverse to exchange tree and cloud positions. You may wish to add window details, or even draw some charts of your own to include scenes special and unique to your child.

BLOCKS: Following specific directions below, work special, detailed blocks first to be sure you have sufficient yarn for specified colors. Then work enough basic blocks, following Basic Chart, for a total of 25 blocks, using remaining colors as desired for houses, doors and paths, varying colors so each block is unique.

  For All Detailed Blocks: Starting at lower edge, with FG (unless otherwise specified), ch 45. **Row 1:** Sc in 2nd ch and each remaining ch across, following first row of desired chart for colors. Follow chart from Y to Z on right-side rows and from Z to Y on wrong-side rows. Use colors you wish in unmarked areas.

  Attach a separate ball of yarn for each large area. To change colors, work last st of old color by drawing up a loop in sc, drop old color on wrong side of work, with new color yo and draw through both loops on hook to complete last st, now work with new color. When last (45th) row of chart is completed, break off.

  When each piece to be appliquéd is completed, weave yarn end into matching color area to conceal it before sewing to block. Follow broken lines of chart for placement of appliquéd and embroidered details. Work special details as follows:

CHART 1. EASTER BUNNY HIDING EGGS To crochet block, work foundation chain as follows: with FG, ch 14; attach GO and ch 8; attach another FG and ch 23.

Bunny: For body, starting at center, ch 5 with white for foundation. **Rnd 1:** Work 2 sc in 2nd ch from hook, sc in next 2 ch, 4 sc in last ch; working on unworked side of foundation, work sc in next 2 ch, work 2 sc in last ch. Sl st to first sc. **Rnd 2:** Work 2 sc in each of first 2 sc (corner), sc in next 2 sc, work 2 sc in each of next 4 sc (corners), sc in next 2 sc, 2 sc in next sc (corner). Sl st to first sc. **Rnd 3:** Sl st in next sc, work leg at first corner as follows: work 2 sc in next sc, ch 1, turn; work 3 more rows on 2 sc, ch 1, turn; work 2 sc in each sc, ch 1, turn sc in each sc. Break off. * Attach W to base of leg; sl st to next corner and work leg as before; repeat from * twice more. For each paw, ch 3 with P. Work 5 sc in 3rd ch from hook. Break off. Bunching edge so piece forms ball, sew paw to end of each leg. Sew body to block, leaving forelegs (top) unattached.

For head, ch 3 with W. **Rnd 1:** Work 6 sc in 3rd ch from hook. **Rnd 2:** Work 2 sc in each sc. **Rnd 3:** Sl st in first 4 sc, for ears work (ch 7, sl st in 2nd ch from hook, sc in next 3 ch, hdc in next 2 ch, skip 1 sc on Rnd 2, sl st in next sc) twice, sl st to end. Break off. With W, ch 3. Work 5 sc in 3rd ch from hook. Break off. Bunch to form ball and sew to head for nose. With P, using small straight stitches, embroider tip of nose and center of ears; with RB, embroider eyes. Sew head to block at top of body, leaving ears unattached.

Basket: With GO, ch 6. **Row 1:** Sc in 2nd ch from hook and each remaining ch. Ch 1, turn. **Row 2:** Work 2 sc in first sc, sc in each remaining sc. Ch 1, turn. **Row 3:** Repeat last row. Ch 14 for handle, sl st in first sc of Row 3 (opposite base of handle), sl st in each ch of handle. Break off. Sew basket to block.

Eggs: Make 8 in assorted bright colors, as follows: ch 3. Work 6 sc in 3rd ch from hook. Break off. Bunching edge to cup piece, sew an egg to underside of one bunny paw, the others as indicated by broken lines on chart.

CHART 2. MARKET LETTERS With R, using straight stitches, embroider letters as shown. If desired, substitute name of child's favorite store.

CHART 3. THE ZOO WITH SNAKE, BEAR, AND PEACOCK *Note:* When crocheting block, on 14th and

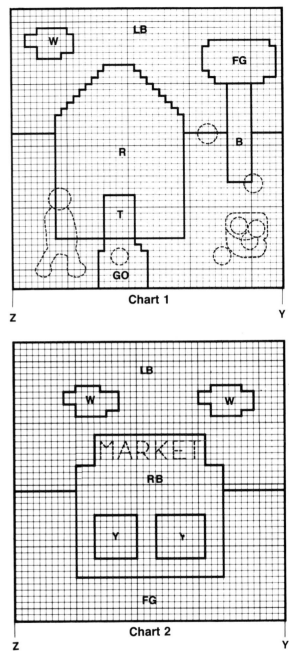

Chart 1

Z   Y

Chart 2

Z   Y

133

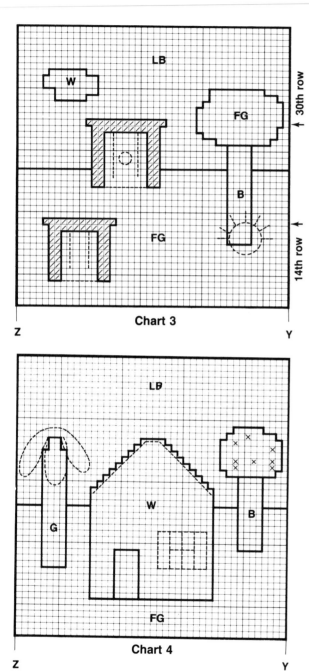

Chart 3

Z   Y

Chart 4

Z   Y

30th rows (wrong side), work sc in front loop only of GO sts at top of cage to form ridge on right side of work.

Snake's Cage: With GO, ch 3. **Row 1:** Sc in 2nd and 3rd ch from hook. Ch 1, turn. Work 8 more rows on 2 sc. Break off. Sew ends and lower edge only of strip to block for cage bottom. Attach GO to free top edge of strip ⅜″ in from one end, ch 10 for bar; sew end of bar to cage top. Attach GO ⅜″ in from other strip end and work another bar.

Bear's Cage: Working in same manner as for snake's cage, make strip 10 rows long for cage bottom and ch 12 for bars.

Snake: With LG, make chain 8″ long for foundation. Sl st in 2nd ch from hook and each remaining ch to last 2 ch, work 2 sc in next ch, work 5 sc in last ch; working on unworked side of foundation, work 2 sc in next ch. Sl st in next ch. Break off. With BK, embroider eyes; make small stitch at front of head, leaving 1″ ends. Knot ends and trim to ½″ for forked tongue. Coil snake around cage bars.

Bear: With B, ch 3. **Rnd 1:** Work 6 sc in 3rd ch from hook. **Rnd 2:** Work 2 sc in each sc. **Rnd 3:** Sc in first sc, work limbs as follows: work (2 sc in next sc, ch 1, turn; sc in each of 2 sc, ch 1, turn; dec 1 sc; sl st into end of first limb row, sc in next 2 sc of circle) 3 times, make 4th limb as before, ending 2 sc in next 2 sc for neck; working head, work (ch 1, turn; sc in each sc) 3 times; ch 1, turn; 2 sc in first sc for ear, ch 1, turn; sc in 2 sc, ch 1, turn; dec 1 sc, sl st into end of first ear row, sc in next 2 sc on head, work ear as before; sl st around edge of bear. Break off. With TA, ch 3. Work 5 sc in 3rd ch from hook. Cupping piece, stuff with scrap of TA yarn and sew to face for snout. With TA, ch 3. **Rnd 1:** Work 6 sc in 3rd ch from hook. **Rnd 2:** Work 2 sc in each sc. Break off. Sew to center of body. With RB, embroider eyes. With limbs and head unattached, sew body to block, under cage bars.

Peacock: For body, ch 3 with RB. **Rnd 1:** Work 6 sc in 3rd ch from hook. **Rnd 2:** Work 2 sc in each sc. For head, ch 1, turn; sc in first 2 sc of Rnd 2, ch 1, turn; sc in 2 sc, ch 1, turn; work 6 sc between 2 sc, sl st to first sc of 6 sc to form cup for head. Break off. With Y, ch 2. Work 2 sc in 2nd ch from hook. Break off. Bunch sts to form ball and attach inside head cup so ball protrudes slightly for beak.

134

For tail feathers, ch 7 with RB for foundation. **Row 1:**
Sc in 2nd ch from hook, * ch 6, sc in 2nd ch from hook
and each remaining ch of ch 6, ch 1, sc in 5 sc, turn, sl st
in 5 sc (feather made), sc in next ch of foundation; repeat
from * until 6 feathers are completed. Break off. With T,
embroider a small satin-stitch circle near top and another
near bottom of each feather. With BK, outline each circle.
Sew tail-feather strip to block, leaving feather tips unattached. Sew body over edge of tail strip, with neck and
head unattached at top.

CHART 4. FLORIDA BUNGALOW WITH ORANGE AND PALM TREES

Palm Fronds: With FG, ch 7. **Row
1:** Work 2 sc in 2nd ch from hook and in each remaining
ch (12 sc). **First Frond:** Sc in first 4 sc. Ch 1, turn. Work
7 more rows on 4 sc. **Next row:** (Dec 1 sc) twice. Break
off. Attach yarn at base of first frond and work 2nd frond
in same manner on center 4 sc, and a 3rd frond on last 4
sc. Bunch foundation ch at top of trunk and sew frond in
place.

Shutter: Make 2. With T, ch 4. **Row 1:** Sc in 2nd ch
from hook and each remaining ch. Ch 1, turn. Work 5
more rows on 3 sc. Break off. Sew shutters in place. Embroider window frames with backstitches.

With shutter color, working through sts of block, crochet a chain, following outline of house top for roof line.

CHART 5. LITTLE RED SCHOOLHOUSE

With FG, ch
20; attach GO and ch 7; attach another FG and ch 18.

CHART 6. HALLOWEEN

With FG, ch 13; attach GO
and ch 8; attach another FG and ch 24.

Jack-o'-lantern: With O, ch 3. **Rnd 1:** Work 6 sc in
3rd ch from hook. **Rnd 2:** Work 2 sc in each sc. **Rnd 3:**
(Sc in next sc, 2 sc in next sc) 6 times. Break off. For stem,
attach LG to edge sc of pumpkin, work 2 sc in same sc.
Ch 1, turn. Dec 1 sc. Break off. With BK, embroider face
on pumpkin. Sew pumpkin in place.

Ghost: With W, ch 3. **Rnd 1:** Work 6 sc in 3rd ch from
hook. **Rnd 2:** Work 2 sc in each sc. Ch 1, do not turn;
continue in rows. **Row 1:** Work 2 sc in first sc, sc in next
sc, 2 sc in next sc, sc in next 2 sc, 2 sc in next sc. Ch 1,
turn. **Row 2:** Work 2 sc in first sc, sc in next 7 sc, 2 sc in
last sc. Ch 1, turn. **Row 3:** Work 2 sc in first sc, sc in next
8 sc. Ch 1, turn. **Row 4:** Sc in first 8 sc. Ch 1, turn. Repeat

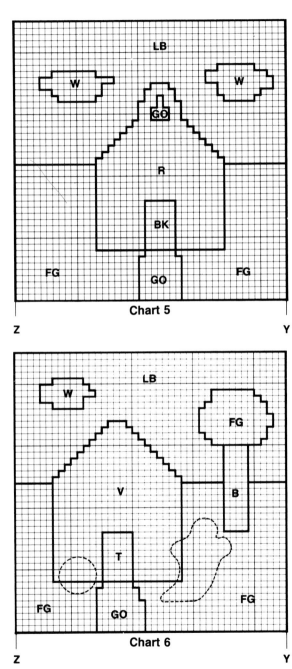

Chart 5

Chart 6

135

last row once more. **Row 6:** Dec 1 sc, sc in next 5 sc, 2 sc in last sc. Ch 1, turn. **Row 7:** Sc in each sc. Ch 1, turn. Repeat last 2 rows once more. **Row 10:** Dec 1 sc, sc in next 5 sc, 3 sc in last sc. Ch 1, turn. **Row 11:** Sc in each sc. Ch 1, turn. **Row 12:** Dec 1 sc, sc in next 7 sc. Break off. With BK, embroider eyes and mouth. Sew ghost to block.

CHART 7. CHURCH With FG, ch 17; attach G and ch 7; attach another FG and ch 21.

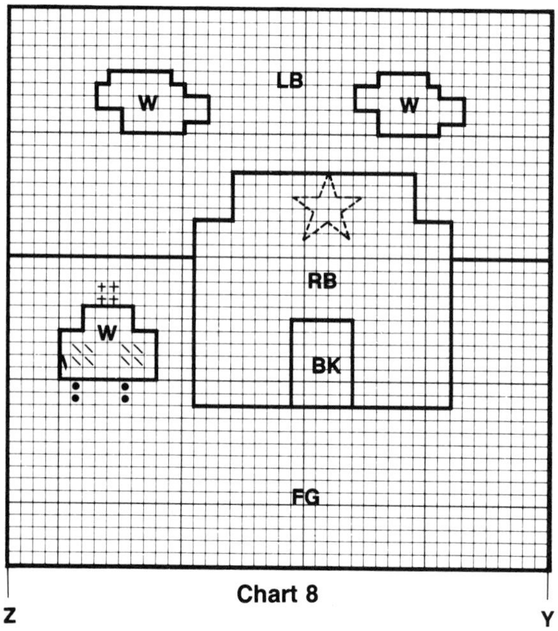

CHART 8. POLICE STATION **Star:** With GO, ch 3. **Rnd 1:** Work 5 sc in 3rd ch from hook. **Rnd 2:** ch 1, work 3 sc in first sc, ch 1, turn; sc in first 2 sc, ch 2, turn; skip 1 sc, sc in last sc, sl st in end of 3-sc row below (first point made) * work next point as follows: work 3 sc in next sc, ch 1, turn; sc in first 2 sc, ch 2, turn; skip 1 sc, sc in last sc, sl st in end of row below; repeat from * 3 times more sl st in first sc of first point. Break off.

CHART 9. FIRE DEPARTMENT With FG, ch 9; attach G and ch 26; attach another FG and ch 10.

Embroidery: With BK, embroider ladder and letters with backstitch.

CHART 10. SEASHORE With GO, ch 45.

Crab (on left): With O, ch 2. **Row 1:** Work 4 sc in 3rd ch from hook. Ch 1, turn. **Row 2:** Work 2 sc in first sc, sc in next 2 sc, 2 sc in last sc. Ch 1, turn. **Row 3:** Sc in first 2 sc, (2 sc in next sc) twice, sc in next 2 sc; ch 4, work 3 sc in 2nd ch from hook for claw. Break off; attach O to first st of Row 3 and make claw as before. With O threaded in tapestry needle, make a small stitch in foundation ch 2, leaving 1″ ends for eye stalks. Make small knot at end of each stalk. With BK, make several tiny stitches over knots for eyes. Sew crab to block, leaving eye stalks and claws unattached.

Conch Shell (center): With P, ch 3. **Row 1:** Work 5 sc in 3rd ch from hook. Ch 1, turn. **Row 2:** Sc in each sc. Ch 1, turn. **Row 3:** Work 2 sc in first sc, sc in 3 sc, 2 sc in last sc. Ch 1, turn. **Row 4:** Sc in each sc. Ch 1, turn. **Row 5:** Sc in 2 sc, 2 sc in next sc, sc in next sc, 2 sc in next sc, sc in next 2 sc. Break off. Roll up from one side to resemble conch shell. Sew to block.

Starfish (on right): With O, work same as Star, Chart 8.

Sailboat: With R, ch 6. **Row 1:** Sc in 2nd ch from hook and each remaining ch. Ch 2, turn. **Row 2:** Work 2 sc in

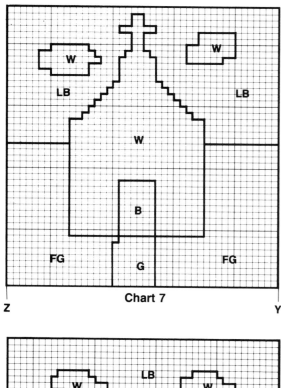

Chart 7

Z   Y

Chart 8

Z   Y

136

2nd ch of ch 2, 2 sc in first sc, sc in next 3 sc, 2 sc in last sc. Ch 1, turn. **Row 3:** Sc in each sc, ending at bow. Break off. Skipping 3 sts at bow, attach W to next sc of Row 3. Ch 2, work 2 sc in 2nd ch of ch 2, now working in back loop only for sail, sc in next 4 sc of boat (6 sc). Ch 1, turn. **Next row:** Sc in first sc, dec 1 sc, sc in 3 sc. Ch 1, turn. **Next row:** Sc in first sc, dec 1 sc, sc in 2 sc. Ch 1, turn. **Next row:** Sc in first sc, dec 1 sc, sc in last sc. Ch 1, turn. **Next row:** Sc in first sc, dec 1 sc. Ch 1, turn. Dec 1 sc. Break off. Sew boat to block.

BASIC CHART: See Note at beginning of instructions. With G, ch 15; attach desired path color and ch 7; attach another FG and ch 23. **Row 1:** Sc in 2nd ch from hook and each remaining ch across, following first row of Basic Chart from Y to Z for colors. On following (wrong side) row, follow chart from Z to Y. (To reverse chart, make foundation ch with 22 FG, 7 path color, and 16 FG. Follow chart from Z to Y on right-side rows, and from Y to Z on wrong-side rows.) When last (45th) row of chart is completed, break off.

ASSEMBLY: Lay out blocks, 5 across and 5 down, in desired arrangement, scattering the special detailed blocks among the basic ones. Join blocks in vertical strips as follows: starting with block at lower left corner, attach W to top right corner of block, right side of work facing you. With W, sc in each of 44 sts across top edge of block. Ch 1, turn. **Next row:** Sc in each sc across. Ch 1, turn. Repeat last row 4 times more. **Next row:** Sc in next 17 sc; break off, attach BK, and sc in next 10 sc; break off, attach W, and sc in last 17 sc. With W only, work 6 more rows on 44 sts. Break off. This completes short joining strip. Sew top edge of strip to bottom edge of next block above. Work short joining strip across top of 2nd block same as before. Continue in this manner, working strip and adding next block above until all 5 blocks for left edge of afghan are joined in vertical strip. Join remaining blocks of afghan in same manner until all blocks are joined into 5 vertical strips of 5 blocks each.

Work long joining strip as follows: starting with left vertical strip, attach W to lower right corner. With right side of work facing you, sc in end of each row along right side edge of block (45 sc), work (13 sc along row ends of next short joining strip, 45 sc along next block) 4 times.

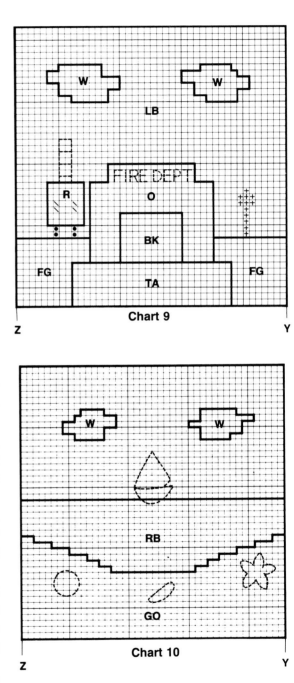

Chart 9

Chart 10

Ch 1, turn. Work 5 more rows of sc with W. **Next row:** Sc 7 W, * 10 BK, 11 W; repeat from *, ending in pattern. Ch 1, turn. With W only, work 6 more rows. Break off. This completes long joining strip. Sew last row of strip to left edge of next vertical strip, matching each st of joining strip to corresponding end of row on vertical strip. Work long joining strip along opposite edge of 2nd vertical strip same as before. Continue in this manner, working joining strip and adding next vertical strip until all 5 strips are joined to form panel.

Work side border along each long side of panel in same manner as long joining strip.

For top border, work into each row end of border and joining strips and in each st of block, working 6 rows with W only. **Next row:** Work 18 W, * 10 BK, 11 W; repeat from * across, ending with 18 W. With W only, work 6 more rows. Break off. Work bottom border in same manner. Sl st in each sc around afghan. Break off.

Dress Macleod Tartan

Crocheted afghan—an interesting and easy project developed by Faye Sharpe of Rokeby, Saskatchewan

To make a "tartan afghan," crochet a filet-mesh foundation with horizontal stripes, then weave in vertical stripes using a tapestry needle threaded with yarn in a contrasting color.

About Faye Sharpe

Faye Sharpe saw a friend's skirt in Canada's Maple Leaf Tartan, borrowed the skirt, and figured out how to make a tartan afghan. "After that I collected all the tartans of Canada's provinces and made an album of them. Then I got some swatches of Scottish tartans, made twenty-two afghans of provincial and Scottish tartans, and displayed them at an art show. I have been making tartans to order ever since." Her tartans have won awards for her—including a first prize at the Saskatchewan Fair. Recently widowed, Faye lives alone on a farm, helping to support herself with her thriving tartan business.

SIZE: About 46″ × 64″, plus 5″ fringe at each end

MATERIALS: Yarn: Knitting worsted, 24½ oz black (color A), 21 oz bright yellow (B), 3½ oz bright red (C); **crochet hook:** size H (5.00 mm), *or the size that gives you the correct gauge;* large-eyed tapestry needle.

GAUGE: 2 sp (meshes) = 1″; 2 rows = 1″.

MESH FOUNDATION: Starting at one end, with color A, ch 186. **Row 1:** Work dc in 6th ch from hook (first sp made), * ch 1, skip next ch, dc in next ch (another sp made); repeat from * across (91 sp). Ch 4, turn. **Row 2:** Skip first dc, * dc in next dc, ch 1; repeat from * across, ending with dc in last dc, ch 1, skip 1 ch of turning ch, dc in next ch of turning ch (91 sp). Ch 4, turn. Repeat Row 2 for pattern of 91 sp on each row throughout, working horizontal stripes as follows: work 2 more rows A, * then work 1 row B, 4 A, 5 B, 1 C, 5 B, 4 A, 1 B, 4 A; repeat from * 4 times more. Break off.

WOVEN VERTICAL STRIPES: *Note:* Work with 3 strands of yarn threaded into large-eyed tapestry needle. Cut yarn lengths long enough (about 80″) to weave through sp with 6″ extending at each end for fringe. Keep yarn strands flat and untwisted as you weave, keeping strands just loose enough to keep foundations from rippling.

Hold work sideways to work along one side (long) edge with 3 strands of B, weaving needle in first sp, out next sp along edge to end, leaving 6″ lengths at each end. In next row of sp, bring needle, with 3 strands of A, *up* from wrong side through first sp, into next sp, out next sp, along row to opposite end, so that yarn strands alternate in and out with previous row to resemble weaving. Continue to alternate weaving of strands in this manner, working 3 more rows A, then (1 row B, 4 A) twice, * 5 B, 1 C, 5 B, (4 A, 1 B) twice, 4 A; repeat from * twice more, ending with 1 B row along opposite side edge of afghan.

FRINGES: See Fringes, page 196. Make fringe along each end of afghan as follows: for each fringe, cut 2 additional 12″ strands of matching yarn, draw strands halfway through edge sp and fold over. Knot these additional strands together with yarn ends of every 2 rows (10 strands per fringe). Trim ends of fringe evenly.

Popcorn Granny

Coverlet in many pieces, crocheted by Joan Stagg of
Watsonville, California

For those who love to make popcorns, here's a
luxurious afghan with lots of thick, puffy ones,
surrounding delicate pink roses.

About Joan Stagg

"I work as a paper carrier for our local newspaper,"
offers this cheerful mother and grandmother. "I have
six hundred customers, and I enjoy serving them."
Joan Stagg calls herself "a novice" at designing
afghans, but it is clear that her natural ability more
than compensates for her lack of experience. Her
sumptuous granny-square afghan displays workman-
ship one normally finds only from a seasoned
needleworker. It is to her credit that even with the
extra bulk contributed by the popcorns, her afghan is
still light and graceful. She says she designs afghans
while watching TV, likes cooking (she was once a
chef), and, with her husband, has marine aquariums
and raises canaries.

SIZE: About 81" × 100"; plus 4½" fringes

MATERIALS: Yarn (see Note below): Knitting worsted, 47 (3½ oz) skeins off-white (MC), 7 peach (A), and 2 green (B); **crochet hook:** size G (4.50 mm) *or the size that gives you the correct gauge.*

Note: If you want to change size of coverlet, these figures will help you: for 1 square you need 75 yd MC, 11 yd A and 13 yd B. Allow 2 skeins MC for joining and tassels.

GAUGE: 4 dc = 1"; square measures 9".

SQUARE: Make 99. **Rose:** Starting at center with color A, ch 3. Join with sl st to form a ring. **Rnd 1:** Ch 3, work 7 dc in ring (8 dc, counting ch 3 as 1 dc); join with sl st to top of ch 3. **Rnd 2:** (Ch 2, sl st in back loop of next st) 8 times (8 loops). **Rnd 3:** In each loop work (sc, 3 dc, sc); join with sl st in first sc (8 petals). **Rnd 4:** (Ch 3, fold next petal forward and sc in Rnd 2 between petals) 7 times; ch 3, sl st at beg of first loop (8 loops made behind petals). **Rnd 5:** In each loop work (sc, hdc, 2 dc, hdc, sc); fasten off.

    Leaves: Rnd 6: With B, sl st in last sc on any petal, ch 3, in same place work (dc, ch 2, 2 dc) for first corner; * ch 2, sc in last sc on next petal, ch 2, in last sc on next petal work (2 dc, ch 2, 2 dc) for another corner; repeat from * twice more, ch 2, sc in last sc on next petal, ch 2; join. Fasten off.

    Finish Square: Rnd 7: With MC, sl st in ch-2 loop before any corner, ch 3, dc in same loop, * dc in each of next 2 corner dc, work corner as before in corner loop, dc in next 2 corner dc, (2 dc in next ch-2 loop) twice; repeat from * twice more, work around corner, 2 dc in last ch-2 loop; join. **Rnd 8:** Ch 3, dc in next 5 dc, * work corner in corner loop, skip next dc, dc in next 11 dc; repeat from * twice more; complete rnd in pattern; join. **Rnd 9 (popcorns):** Ch 4, work first popcorn as follows: holding back on hook the last loop of each tr, work 4 tr in same place as sl st, yo, draw through all 5 loops on hook (first popcorn completed); dc in next 2 dc, make another popcorn as follows: holding back on hook the last loop of each tr, work 5 tr in next dc, yo, draw through all 6 loops on hook (another popcorn completed); dc in next 2 dc, * popcorn in next dc, skip next dc, work corner in corner loop, skip next dc, (popcorn in next dc, dc in next 2 dc) 4 times;

repeat from * twice more; complete rnd in pattern (5 popcorn on each side); join to top of popcorn. **Rnd 10 (popcorns):** Ch 3, dc in next dc, (popcorn in next dc, dc in next popcorn, dc in next dc) twice, * popcorn in next dc, work corner in corner loop, skip next dc, (popcorn in next dc, dc in next popcorn, dc in next dc) 5 times; repeat from * twice more; complete rnd in pattern, ending with popcorns; join (6 popcorn on each side). **Rnd 11:** Ch 3, dc in next 10 sts, * work corner in corner loop, skip next dc, dc in next 19 sts; repeat from * twice more; complete rnd in pattern; join (23 dc on each side). **Rnd 12:** Ch 3, dc in next 12 dc, * work corner in corner loop, skip next dc, dc in next 22 dc; repeat from * twice more; complete rnd in pattern; join (26 dc on each side). Fasten off.

FINISHING: Joining: Working in back loop of sts as before, hold 2 squares wrong sides together, matching corners. Make loop on hook with MC, join a pair of ch sts as follows: insert hook in 2nd ch st of a corner loop on front square and into matching ch st on back square, complete sl st, (sl st in next pair of dc on squares) 26 times; sl st in next pair of ch sts on corner loops; fasten off. Join squares in 9 strips of 11 squares each. Join strips, side by side, in same way.

Border. With MC, work row of dc across one end of coverlet (top edge). Fasten off. **Fringe:** See Fringes, page 196. For each fringe, cut 6 strands MC 9″ long. Make a fringe in every other dc along sides and lower edge.

Striped Odyssey

A second-prize winner, crocheted by Linda Stephens of Cridersville, Ohio

Travel an adventurous road—with a new pattern at each turn—to re-create this imaginative coverlet.

About Linda Stephens

Artist-calligrapher Linda Stephens started with a desire to crochet an afghan with each band "as diverse as possible. I experimented with carrying my colors across and crocheting over them until I needed a certain color, and then picking it up and making a stitch with it. After working about twelve inches I saw that by working tighter I was revealing the pattern much better. So after putting on an additional three or four feet, I took out the first twelve inches, and carefully pulled yarn through the loops made when I removed the beginning." In all, Linda used thirty-three colors and shades—first from her leftover yarn collection, then from "a merry spree of yarn shopping" to find the analogous colors she envisioned in her design. Her results are extraordinary: although each band in her afghan is unique, the bands work together to produce a kaleidoscopic effect that is compelling.

SIZE: About 60″ × 63″, plus 6″ fringe

MATERIALS: Yarn: Knitting worsted, about 90 oz in various colors (designer used 33 colors and shades, including 14 oz dark brown, color Z, for borders); **crochet hook:** size G (4.50 mm) *or the size that gives you the correct gauge.*

GAUGE: 9 sc = 2″; 13 rows = 3″.

Notes: This afghan is made of 29 patterned stripes worked in sc. All rows are worked from the right side. For each stripe, the designer used progressive shades of one color for some stripes, contrasting colors for others. On the charts, symbols for A, B, and so forth represent different colors on different stripes. Use one color (Z) for borders between stripes.

A 6″ fringe is left at each end of each row. When working with two colors, start both together, leaving 6″ ends for fringe; as you work row, hold color not in use behind top of row and enclose it in sts of other color to carry it across. To change colors in pattern, work off last 2 loops of last sc of old color with next color.

To follow charts, always read repeat from right to left, ending pattern as established. Some patterns do not repeat evenly.

AFGHAN: With Z, ch 274. **Row 1 (right side):** Sc in 2nd ch from hook and in each ch across (273 sc). Cut yarn, leaving 6″ end. **Row 2 (right side):** Leaving 6″ end, make loop on hook; following Chart 1, with right side of work facing you draw up loop in first sc, yo and draw through both loops on hook (first sc made); sc in next sc and in each sc across; fasten and cut yarn, leaving 6″ end. Complete Chart 1. With Z work 1 row for border. Continue following charts in numerical order, working 1 row with Z between narrow stripes that are up to 8 rows wide, and 1 row Z, 1 row any color, 1 row Z before and after wider stripes. (*Note:* When all rows are worked from same side, the edges tend to slant from left to right. To compensate, on the Z rows that are at least 8 rows apart, dec 1 st at beginning of row and inc 1 st near end of same row. *To dec,* draw up loop in each of next 2 sts, yo and draw through all 3 loops on hook. *To inc,* work 2 sc in 1 sc.)

When 29th stripe is completed, work 1 row with Z. Fasten off.

FRINGE: Knot together every four 6″ yarn ends along each side edge, making knots close to afghan.

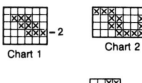

Chart 1 — 2

Chart 2

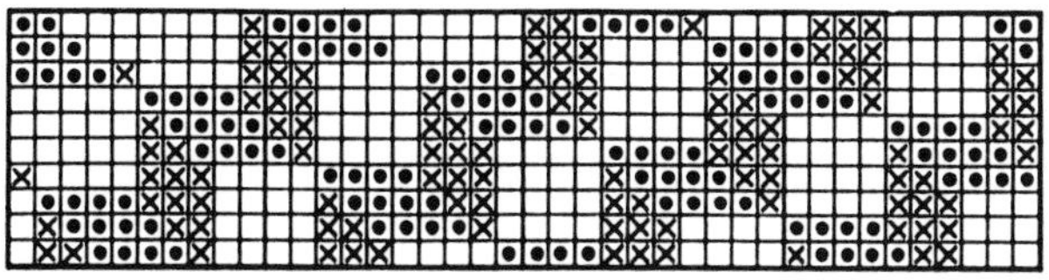

Chart 3

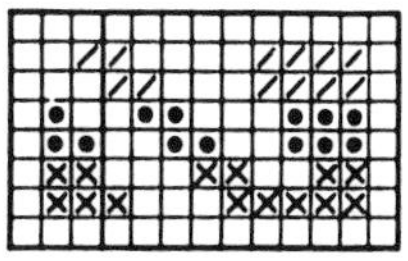

Chart 4

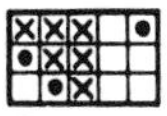

Chart 5

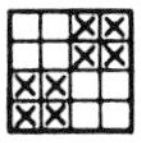

Chart 7

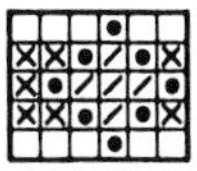

Chart 8

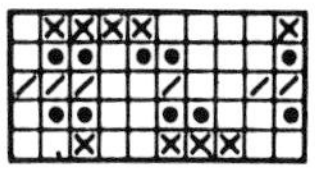

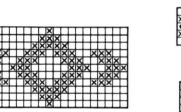

Chart 6

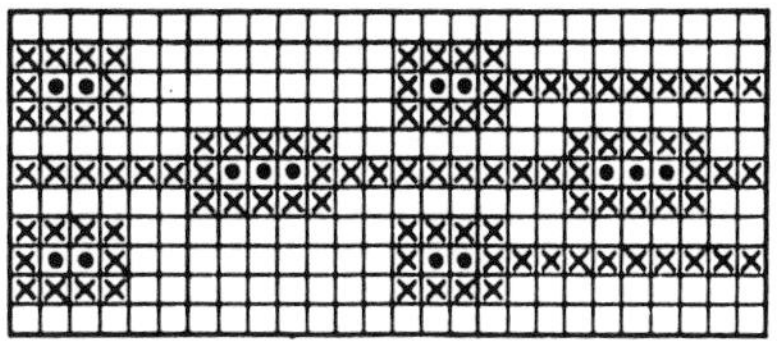

Chart 9

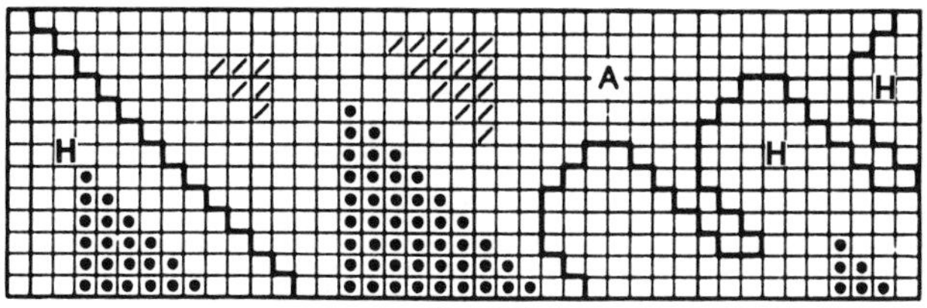

Chart 10

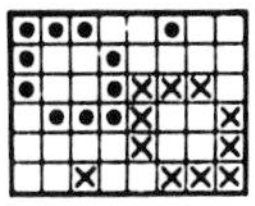

Chart 11

Chart 12

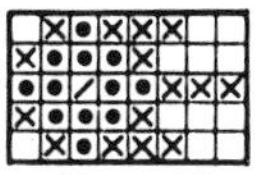

Chart 13

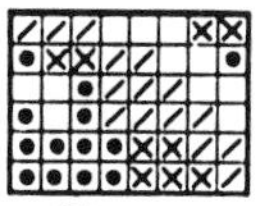

Chart 14

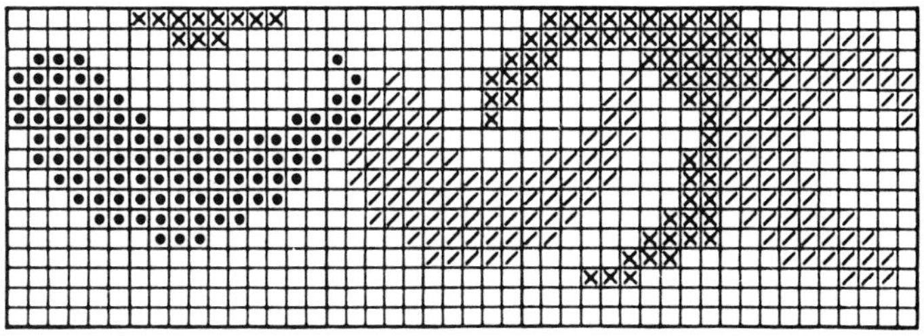

Chart 15

Chart 16

Chart 17

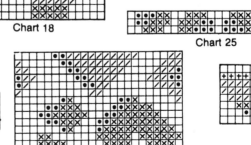

Chart 18

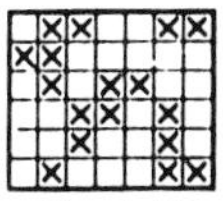

Chart 19

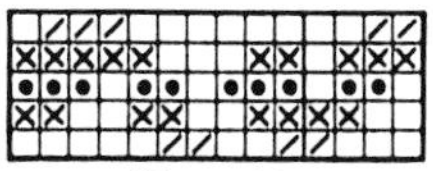

Chart 20

Chart 25

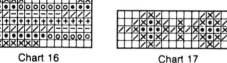

Chart 21

Chart 23

Chart 22

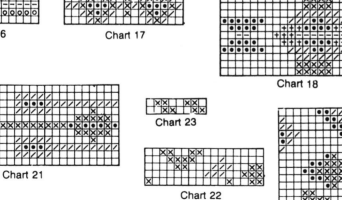

Chart 24

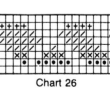

Chart 26

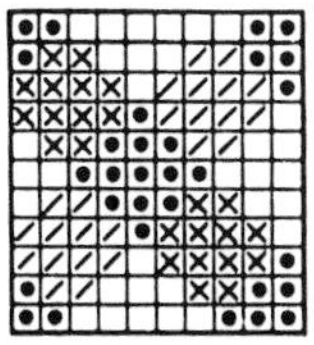

Chart 27

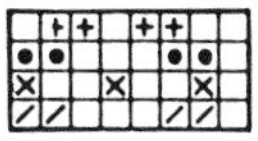

Chart 28

Chart 29

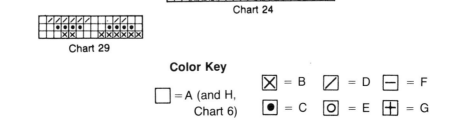

Color Key

☐ = A (and H, Chart 6)

☒ = B ◪ = D ⊟ = F

● = C ⊡ = E ⊞ = G

149

Southwestern Geometric

Coverlet crocheted with a special technique for making fringe, by Mary Carol Sumner of Sumner, Illinois

Variegated yarns in combination with raised-pattern stitches create a decorative Navajo-style design.

About Mary Carol Sumner

"When I was a child," Mary Carol Sumner recalls, "my mother used to crochet rugs made from old clothes." This may explain Mary's preference for crochet over other types of needlework, though she admits to "having tried everything in the book." Even though she began her contest entry before the onset of her late husband's illness, she especially recalls those weeks when it went back and forth with her to the hospital. "I slept under it at night and worked on it during the day when I could. The nurses, who were very complimentary, said they were going to steal it. Joe would tell them, 'You wouldn't do that, that one is mine.' " Of the more than a dozen afghans Mary has crocheted, Mary says, this is her "special one." So for now she plans to keep it, and eventually give it to her son.

SIZE: About 54″ (plus 3½″ fringes) × 72″

MATERIALS: Yarn: See Note below. Knitting worsted, 24 oz brown variegated (MC), 5 colors to match colors of variegated yarn: 16 oz dark brown (color A), 12 oz cinnamon brown (B), 4 oz each burnt orange (C) and light coral (D), 14 oz natural white (E); **crochet hook:** size H (5.00 mm) *or the size that gives you the correct gauge.*

Note: Yarn colors: Original afghan was made with yarn colors listed above. To make afghan with different colors, choose desired variegated yarn (MC) and 5 colors that match the shadings of the yarn. Use the darkest shade for color A and grade to the lightest shade, E.

Hint: If you find work edge becoming slanted, you can compensate by periodically skipping first st of row and increasing at end of same row to keep edges straight.

GAUGE: 9 sts = 2″; 4 rows = 1″.

AFGHAN: Starting at one end, with color A, ch 245. **Row 1:** Sc in 2nd ch from hook and in each remaining ch across (244 sc). Break off, leaving a 4″ end for side edge fringe. Do not turn work. **Row 2:** Leaving 4″ end for fringe, make slip knot on hook (as if to start foundation ch), sc in back loop of first sc and in each sc across. Break off, leaving 4″ end for fringe. With right side of work *always* facing you and leaving a 4″ yarn end at each side, repeat Row 2, working until there are 7 rows of A, then work rows as follows: 3 MC, 7 A, 4 B, 1 E, 3 MC, 2 E, 4 MC, 3 E, 1 C, 3 E, 4 MC, 2 E, 3 MC, 1 E, 4 B, 4 A, 1 E, 4 A, 4 D, 1 E, 18 MC, 1 E, 4 A, 2 E, 5 B, 4 C, 3 A, 1 E, 3 C, 5 B, 14 MC.

Now work raised diamond design rows as follows: **Row 1:** With A, sc in first 28 sc, * work raised dc as follows: yo and draw up a loop in unworked front loop of sc 2 rows below next sc, (yo and draw through 2 loops on hook) twice—raised dc made; skip sc behind raised dc, sc in next 40 sc; repeat from * 4 times more, work raised dc below next sc, sc in last 10 sc. **Row 2:** With E, sc in first 27 sc, * work raised dc 2 rows below next sc, sc in back loop of raised dc, work raised dc 2 rows below next sc, sc in next 38 sc; repeat from * across, ending with sc in last 9 sc. **Row 3:** With D, sc in first 26 sc, * work raised dc below next sc, sc in next 3 sc, work raised dc below next sc, sc in next 36 sc; repeat from * across, ending with sc in last 8 sc. **Row 4:** With E, * sc to within 1 st of next

152

raised dc, work raised dc below next sc, sc to next raised dc, sc in this raised dc, work raised dc below next sc; repeat from * across, ending with sc to end. Continue in this manner, working 2 sc more between raised dc in each diamond, and working colors as follows: 1 row B, 1 E, and 1 A. **Row 8:** With E, * sc to next raised A dc, sc in this dc, work raised dc in unworked loop of raised E dc below, sc to within 1 sc of next raised dc, work raised dc in raised E dc below, sc in raised A dc; repeat from * across, sc to end. **Row 9:** With B, * sc to next raised dc, sc in raised dc, work raised dc in unworked loop of sc 2 rows below next dc, sc to within 1 sc of next raised dc, work raised dc below next sc, sc in raised dc of previous row; repeat from * across, sc to end. There are 2 sc fewer between raised dc of each diamond. Continue in this manner, working colors as follows: 1 row E, 1 D, and 1 E. **Row 13:** With A, * sc to next raised dc, sc in raised dc, work raised dc in next sc (between raised dc of previous row), sc in raised dc of previous row; repeat from * across—6 diamonds formed by raised dc.

Working in back loop only of each st, work 14 more sc rows with MC.

Now work raised diamond design rows again as follows: **Row 1:** With A, sc in first 10 sc, * work raised dc in sc 2 rows below next sc, sc in next 40 sc; repeat from * 4 times more, work raised dc below next sc, sc in last 28 sc. **Row 2:** With E, sc in first 9 sc, * work raised dc below next sc, sc in back loop of raised dc of previous row, work raised dc below next sc, sc in next 38 sc; repeat from * across, ending with sc in last 27 sc. With position of diamonds established, work diamonds in same manner as before, keeping same color sequence. When diamonds are completed with A row, work sc rows as follows: 14 MC, 5 B, 3 D, 1 E, 3 A, 4 C, 5 B, 2 E, 4 A, 1 E, 18 MC, 1 E, 4 D, 4 A, 1 E, 4 A, 4 B, 1 E, 4 MC, 2 E, 3 MC, 3 E, 1 C, 3 E, 3 MC, 2 E, 4 MC, 1 E, 4 B, 7 A, 3 MC, 7 A. Break off.

FINISHING: Trim yarn ends at beginning and end of each row to an even 3½".

Cat Got In the Paint

"Quilt" worked in an easy knitting pattern by
Lynn Swereda of Carman, Manitoba

The traditional bear- or cat-paw quilt pattern also
makes a stunning knitted spread.

About Lynn Swereda

The daughter of a Canadian bush pilot, Lynn Swereda grew up in many places. One was an Icelandic fishing community on the shores of Lake Winnipeg. Another time she lived near an Indian reservation and often had to rely on a canoe or dog team to get her to school. Her "country quilt" afghan is a collaboration between Lynn and her older daughter, Coral. They decided a quilt pattern would be great, and picked this particular one because of Lynn's fondness for cats (she has five). She has "made things galore for family and friends and for sale" and won ribbons at the local fair. This afghan she'll keep for her own couch back, for use during cold prairie evenings.

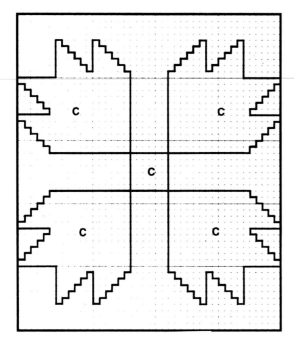

Each square = one stitch

SIZE: About 58″ square

MATERIALS: Yarn: Knitting worsted, 30 oz white, small amounts of assorted colors (see Note below); **knitting needles:** 1 pair size 8 (5.00 mm) *or the size that gives you the correct gauge;* tapestry needle; size G or H crochet hook (optional).

GAUGE: 5 sts = 1″; 6 rows = 1″.

Note: The design areas on the original afghan were worked in red, wine, black, brown, yellow, blues, and greens. Rather than try to duplicate the colors exactly, you may wish to use yarn remnants already on hand or easily (and cheaply) obtained from knitting friends or local yarn shops. Be sure to have enough yarn to complete chart with one color each time you work the design.

Carry color not in use loosely across back of work, catching carried yarn every 2 or 3 sts to avoid long loops on reverse. When changing colors, twist yarns by bringing new color under color you have been working with, to avoid holes in work.

AFGHAN STRIPS: Make 6. Starting at one end, with white, cast on 50 sts. Work in stockinette st for 6 rows. Attach a colored yarn and, continuing to work in stockinette st, follow chart for design, working all C areas with colored yarn and all background sts with white. * When last row of chart is completed, break off colored yarn. With white only, work 6 rows. Attach a different-color yarn and follow chart for design as before. Repeat from * until 7 designs are completed, working colors randomly. Work 6 rows of white. Bind off all sts.

ASSEMBLY: Arrange strips side by side, so that colored designs form a pleasant random pattern. Neatly sew strips together with yarn along side edges. If desired, crochet a row of sc all around edge of afghan with white, working 3 sc at each corner, and spacing sts to keep edges flat and smooth.

Pastel Granny

Coverlet of crocheted squares (a very portable project)
by Charlotte Tartaglino of Roselle, New Jersey

Shades of pale blue, lavender, and rose ombré create a
light and lacy Victorian patchwork.

About Charlotte Tartaglino

Executive secretary, mother of three, and grandmother
of one, Charlotte Tartaglino says, "I find crochet to be
a creative and relaxing outlet and, with my busy
schedule, somewhat of a challenge." Charlotte always
has a take-along project with her—one that she can
work on during a lunch hour, in a waiting room, or in
the evenings as time permits. Her beautiful granny was
designed to match the bedroom decor of the Victorian
home where her daughter and son-in-law will live when
they return from a two-year assignment in Hong Kong.
Says Charlotte, "The effect I wanted was that of softness,
serenity—reminiscent of a more romantic era."

SIZE: 61″ × 85″

MATERIALS: Yarn: Brushed acrylic knitting-worsted-weight yarn, about 10 oz white (MC), about 25 oz assorted colors: pale blue (color A), pink (B), rose (C), lavender (D), and rose ombré (E); **crochet hook:** size H (5.00 mm) *or size that gives you correct gauge.*

GAUGE: 7 sts = 2″. Each square measures 6″.

Note: Make 70 squares from random assortment of stitch patterns (below). They are crocheted together with loops of MC to form a rectangle 7 squares by 10 squares, then border is added.

BASIC GRANNY SQUARE: Note: Intructions are written for color change on each row. When working variations in which same color is used for more than one row, sl st to next corner space instead of fastening off. To change colors within row, cut and join colors as needed.

Work with any colors. Starting at center, ch 6. Join with sl st to form ring. **Rnd 1:** Ch 3, work 2 dc in ring, ch 3, work (3 dc in ring, ch 3) 3 times; join with sl st in top of ch 3. Fasten off. **Rnd 2:** Work first corner as follows: sl st in next ch-3 sp, ch 3 (counts as 1 dc), work (2 dc, ch 3, 3 dc) in same sp (first corner made); ch 1, * work (3 dc, ch 3, 3 dc) in next sp (corner made); ch 1, repeat from * twice more; join. Fasten off. **Rnd 3:** Work first corner in next corner sp, ch 1, 3 dc in next sp, ch 1, work (corner in next corner sp, ch 1, 3 dc in next sp, ch 1) 3 times; join. Fasten off. **Rnd 4:** Work first corner in next corner sp, ch 1, work (3 dc in next sp, ch 1) twice; * corner in next corner sp, ch 1, work (3 dc in next sp, ch 1) twice; repeat from * twice more; join. Fasten off. **Rnd 5:** Work as for Rnd 4, working 1 more (3 dc in next sp, ch 1) on each side between corners.

Variations of Basic Square: Work 5 rnds on each square in colors as follows: **No. 1:** B, D, MC, A, B. **No. 2:** D, MC, E, B, A. **No. 3:** C, E, B, MC, D. **No. 4:** MC, A, B, E, D. **No. 5:** C, 3 MC, A. **No. 6:** MC, 4 A. **No. 7:** MC, 4 D, **No. 8:** C, 2 MC, 2 D. **No. 9:** MC, 4 C. **No. 10: Rnd 1:** B. **Rnds 2 through 4:** Work corners with MC, ch 1's and 3-dc groups with A. **Rnd 5:** A. **No. 11:** Work as for No. 10, substituting D for A. **No. 12: Rnd 1:** A. **Rnd 2:** MC. **Rnd 3:** C. **Rnd 4:** Work corners with MC, ch 1's and 3-dc groups with C. **Rnd 5:** C.

in edge of 2nd square; repeat from * along adjacent side, working in each corresponding loop to next corner, work joining in corner as before. Continue to join adjacent sides of squares in same manner until all squares are joined.

BORDER: Rnd 1: With right side facing you, with MC, work 5 sc in each loop and sc in each sc around; sl st in first sc. **Rnd 2:** Ch 3, dc in each sc around, working 5 dc in each corner sc; sl st in top of ch 3. **Rnd 3:** * Ch 5, skip next 2 dc, sc in next dc; repeat from * around, sl st in sl st. **Rnd 4:** Sl st in next ch, * ch 5, sc in next loop; repeat from * around; sl st in first sl st. **Rnd 5:** * Ch 6, sc in 3rd ch from hook for picot, ch 3, sc in next sp (picot sp made); repeat from * around, working picot sp 5 times in each corner sp; sl st in first sl st. Fasten off.

Star Granny

Coverlet worked in squares (a portable project) by
Marion Tuthill of Crown Point, New York

Pieced-quilt pattern of eight-pointed stars and scattered
roses produces a bold graphic.

About Marion Tuthill

Crafts have always been a welcomed friend to Marion
Tuthill, and now that she is widowed and caring for
her aged mother, she fills long winter evenings with
new projects that, in Marion's words, "just pop into
my mind." In this case, she remembers a star-quilt
pattern of her grandmother's called "Texas Star." As a
logical extension of the small items and doilies that
Marion was accustomed to making, she began
experimenting with granny-square designs, sewing
them together like her grandmother's piecework. After
laying out the gray and white squares in the star
pattern, Marion felt that colored flowers were needed
to add contrast and texture. Over the years, Marion's
many crochet items have been made as gifts for friends
and family. This being no exception, she plans to give
the star granny to her daughter.

SIZE: Blocked, about 72″ square

MATERIALS: Yarn: Knitting worsted, 46 oz white (color A), 35 oz gray (B), 4 oz each pink (C), and dark red (D), 2 oz cream (E); **crochet hook:** size G (4.50 mm) *or the size that gives you the correct gauge.*

GAUGE: Each square measures about 5½″ square.

Note: Entire afghan is worked with three types of squares: One-Color Squares, Rose Squares, and Two-Color Squares, which are divided into 2 colors diagonally and form the points of the stars.

ONE-COLOR SQUARE: Make 32 with color A, 16 with B. All rnds are worked from right side. Starting at center, ch 4; join with sl st to form ring. **Rnd 1:** Ch 3 (count as first dc), work 2 dc in ring, * ch 3 for corner sp, work 3 dc in ring; repeat from * twice more, join as follows: ch 1, work dc in top of first ch 3 (4th corner sp made). **Rnd 2:** Ch 3, 2 dc in same corner sp, ch 2, * work (3 dc, ch 3, 3 dc) all in next corner sp, ch 2; repeat from * around, ending last repeat with 3 dc in first corner sp; join as for Rnd 1. **Rnd 3:** Ch 3, 2 dc in same corner sp, * ch 2, 3 dc in next ch-2 sp, ch 2, work (3 dc, ch 3, 3 dc) in next corner sp; repeat from * around, ending last repeat with 3 dc in first corner sp; join as before. **Rnds 4 and 5:** Work as for Rnd 3, repeating (3 dc in next ch-2 sp, ch 2) across each side to next corner. Fasten off. There are twenty 3-dc groups on last rnd.

TWO-COLOR SQUARE: Make 64. Starting at center with A, ch 4; join to form ring. **Rnd 1 (right side):** With A, ch 3 (count as first dc), in ring work 2 dc, ch 3 (corner), 3 dc, ch 3 (corner), drop A to wrong side; with B, sl st in ring, ch 3 and draw loop through A loop on hook to join colors; with B, in ring work 2 dc, ch 3 (corner), 3 dc, ch 1, dc in top of ch 3 at beginning to join rnd and form last corner. Ch 3, turn. **Rnd 2:** Work 2 dc over ch 1 of same corner sp, ch 2, work (3 dc, ch 3, 3 dc) all in next sp, ch 2; working over strand A, work 3 dc in next sp, ch 3, drop B to wrong side; with A, sl st in same ch-3 sp, ch 3, draw loop through B loop on hook, work 2 dc in same ch-3 sp (corner completed), ch 2, work (3 dc, ch 3, 3 dc) in next ch-3 sp, ch 2, 3 dc in first corner sp (over dc), ch 1, dc in top of ch 3. Ch 3, turn. **Rnd 3:** Work 2 dc in same corner sp, ** ch 2,

165

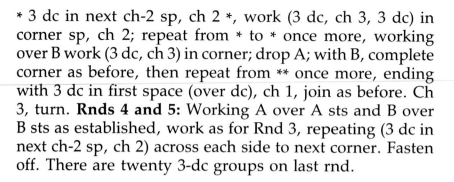

* 3 dc in next ch-2 sp, ch 2 *, work (3 dc, ch 3, 3 dc) in corner sp, ch 2; repeat from * to * once more, working over B work (3 dc, ch 3) in corner; drop A; with B, complete corner as before, then repeat from ** once more, ending with 3 dc in first space (over dc), ch 1, join as before. Ch 3, turn. **Rnds 4 and 5:** Working A over A sts and B over B sts as established, work as for Rnd 3, repeating (3 dc in next ch-2 sp, ch 2) across each side to next corner. Fasten off. There are twenty 3-dc groups on last rnd.

ROSE SQUARE: Make 32. All rnds are worked from right side. Starting at center with E, ch 4. **Rnd 1 (right side):** Ch 1, work 8 sc in ring; join with sl st to back loop of first sc; fasten off. **Rnd 2:** Join C to back loop of any sc; ch 3 (count as 1 dc), work 3 dc in back loop of same sc, remove hook from loop, insert hook from front through top of ch 3 and through dropped loop, yo and draw yarn through (popcorn made); ch 2, * work popcorn of 4 dc in back loop of next sc, ch 2; repeat from * around; join with sl st to top of first ch 3. Fasten off. **Rnd 3:** Join D in any ch-2 sp, work popcorn and ch 3 in each sp around; join. (*Note:* Piece will tend to cup.) Fasten off. **Rnd 4:** Join A in any ch-3 sp, ch 3, 2 dc in same sp, * ch 2, work (3 dc, ch 3, 3 dc) all in next sp (corner), ch 2, 3 dc in next ch-3 sp; repeat from * around, ending last repeat with corner, ch 2; join with sl st to top of ch 3. Fasten off. **Rnd 5:** Join B in any ch-2 sp before a corner, ch 3 and 2 dc in same sp, ch 2, ** work (3 dc, ch 3, 3 dc) in corner sp, ch 2, * 3 dc in next sp, ch 2; repeat from * to next corner; repeat from ** around, ending last repeat with ch 2, sl st in top of ch 3. Fasten off. **Rnd 6:** With A, repeat Rnd 5. Fasten off. There are twenty 3-dc groups on last rnd.

FINISHING: Following photograph for placement (since bottom corners are hidden, turn book upside down to complete corners), assemble squares, sewing through back loops of sts with A. **Border:** With right side of work facing you, using B, sc in back loop of each st around afghan, working 3 sc at each corner. Fasten off.

Flower Baskets

Bedspread in afghan stitch and cross-stitch by
Mildred Viger of Lincoln Park, Michigan

Fringe-finished flower-basket afghan has a light,
luxurious look that would grace any room in the
house. Small units make this a pleasant take-along
project.

About Mildred Viger

Of the attributes that Mildred Viger has gained from
mothering six children, patience and a willingness to
experiment have proved the most helpful to her
needlework. She admits to having tried at least five
variations before selecting this one for her afghan.
Says Mildred, "I wanted to make something different,
something no one else had." Combining a simple
cross-stitched design with textural afghan stitches—
plain, seed, and bobble—she created a charming
collection of twenty little straw baskets, each over-
flowing with freshly gathered flowers in a variety of
colors. Her efforts have been royally rewarded, since
her afghan was also judged Best of Show at the
Michigan State Fair.

SIZE: About 52" × 65", plus 4" fringe

MATERIALS: Yarn: Knitting worsted, 90 oz off-white, 2 oz each gold, yellow, pale yellow, dark avocado green, medium green, light green, small amounts of assorted flower colors in dark, medium, and light shades (see Embroidery, below); **hooks:** 14"-long afghan hook and crochet hook, both size G (4.50 mm) *or the size that gives you the correct gauge;* tapestry needle.

GAUGE: In plain afghan st, 9 sts = 2"; 7 rows = 2". Finished block measures about 12½" square.

PATTERN STITCHES: *Plain Afghan Stitch.* See Plain Afghan Stitch, page 195.

Seed Stitch: **Row 1:** Work same as for plain afghan stitch. **Row 2:** Work afghan purl st as follows: holding yarn in front of work, insert hook in front thread of 2nd vertical bar and draw up a loop (see diagram), * work afghan knit st as follows: with yarn in back of work insert hook in next vertical bar and draw up a loop (same as for plain afghan st), work afghan purl st in next vertical bar; repeat from * across. Work off loops as for first row. **Row 3:** Work afghan knit st in 2nd vertical bar, * work afghan purl st in next vertical bar, afghan knit st in next vertical bar; repeat from * across. Repeat Rows 2 and 3 for pattern st, always working a knit st above a purl st of previous row and a purl st above a knit st.

Bobble: Work afghan knit st in next vertical bar, then in *same* vertical bar work (yo, afghan knit st) 3 times, yo and carefully draw through first 7 loops on hook. As you work back across row, work off bobble-st loop same as for other loops.

BLOCK: Make 20. With off-white and afghan hook, ch 50. Work in seed st pattern on 49 sts for 5 rows. **Row 6:** Work seed st across first 16 sts, * bobble in next vertical bar, plain (knit) afghan st in next 2 bars; repeat from * 4 times more; bobble in next bar, work seed st to end, keeping continuity of pattern as established. Work off loops (6 bobbles on row). **Row 7:** Work seed st across first 15 sts (to within 1 st before bobble), work plain afghan st across 18 sts (to next st after last bobble), work seed st to end. Work off loops. (*Note:* Always work off loops to complete each row.) **Row 8:** Work seed st across first 14 sts (to within 1 st before first plain st), bobble in next bar, plain afghan

Afghan Purl Stitch

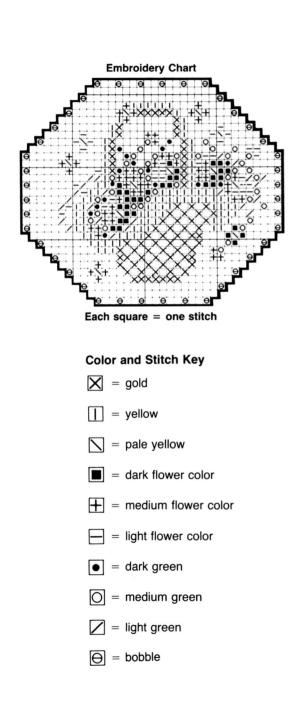

Embroidery Chart

Each square = one stitch

Color and Stitch Key

ⓧ = gold

Ⅱ = yellow

◪ = pale yellow

◼ = dark flower color

⊞ = medium flower color

⊟ = light flower color

• = dark green

Ⓞ = medium green

◩ = light green

⊖ = bobble

st across 18 sts (to last plain st of previous row), bobble in next bar, work seed st to end. **Row 9:** Work seed st to within 1 st before bobble, place marker in work just after last bar, work plain afghan st to next st after last bobble (4 more plain sts than on previous row), place marker in work, beginning with p st work seed st to end. **Row 10:** Work seed st, ending in 2nd st before marker, work bobble in next bar, work plain afghan st to next marker, work bobble in next bar, beginning with p st work seed st to end. **Rows 11 through 16:** Repeat Rows 9 and 10 three times more. **Row 17:** Work seed st across first 6 sts to bobble, plain afghan st across 36 sts (ending over bobble), work seed st to end. **Row 18:** Work seed st across first 6 sts, bobble in next bar, plain afghan st across next 34 sts, bobble in next bar, work seed st to end. **Rows 19 through 26:** Repeat Rows 17 and 18 four times more. **Row 27:** Work seed st to bobble, seed st above bobble (1 more seed st than on previous row), plain afghan st to next bobble, beginning with p st in bobble work seed st to end. **Row 28:** Work seed st across seed sts of previous row, seed st in next st (1 more seed st), bobble in next bar, plain afghan st across to within last 2 plain sts of previous row, bobble in next bar, beginning with p st work seed st in last plain st and in seed sts to end. **Rows 29 through 34:** Repeat rows 27 and 28 three times more. **Row 35:** Repeat Row 27. **Row 36:** Work 1 more seed st than on previous row, bobble in next bar, * plain afghan st in next 2 bars, bobble in next bar; repeat from * 4 times more, work seed st to end. Work 5 more rows of seed st. Sl st in each st across. Break off.

Block Border: Rnd 1: With right side of work facing you, attach off-white to one corner. Using crochet hook, * work 41 sc evenly spaced along edge to next corner, ch 2; repeat from * 3 times more around block. Sl st in first sc. **Rnd 2:** Ch 2, work first cluster st as follows: (yo, draw up loop at base of ch 2) 3 times, yo and draw through all loops on hook, ch 1 to fasten (first cluster st made), * skip 1 sc, make cluster st in next sc as follows: in next sc (yo and draw up a loop) 3 times in same st, yo and draw through all loops on hook, ch 1 to fasten (cluster st made); repeat from * around, working (cluster st, ch 2, cluster st) over each corner ch 2. End with cluster st and ch over last corner ch 2. Sl st in first cluster st (22 cluster sts on each side). **Rnd 3:** Ch 1, working in front loop only of each st, sc in top of each cluster st, in each ch 1, and in each ch of corner ch 2 (rnd forms a ridge around block). Break off.

EMBROIDERY: See Cross-Stitch over Afghan Stitch, page 195. Following chart and color key, embroider basket design on plain-afghan-st area at center of each block. On each block, flowers were embroidered in dark, medium, and light shades of one color, such as rose, violet, orange, blue, gold, pink, red, aqua, salmon, yellow, turquoise, and so on. You can use a different flower color for each block or, if colors are limited, make several blocks of each color, or even all blocks with the same flower color.

ASSEMBLY: Arranging colors as desired, join blocks to form panel 4 blocks wide by 5 blocks long as follows: hold 2 blocks with right sides together. Working through unworked back loops of Rnd 2 sts (at base of ridge), crochet blocks together with sl st along one edge. Continue to join blocks to form vertical or horizontal strips, then crochet strips together to form afghan.

FINISHING: Afghan Border: With right side facing you, attach yarn to one corner of afghan. **Rnd 1:** Working through unworked back of Rnd 2 sts (at base of ridge), ch 2, work first cluster st as for Block Border, * skip 1 unworked loop, work cluster st in next loop; repeat from * around, working (cluster st, ch 2, cluster st) at each corner. End with cluster st and ch 2 at last corner. Sl st to first cluster st. **Rnd 2:** Ch 1, working in front loop only of each st, sc in each st around, forming ridge around afghan. Break off.

FRINGE: See Fringes, page 196. Using four 8″ strands of off-white, make a fringe in every 3rd sc across ends of afghan.

   Note: A single block, with one or more rows of border all around, would make a handsome pillow top to match your afghan.

Pineapple Aran

A third-prize winner, knit by Marie Wagner of La Jolla, California

A "touch of the Irish" is blended with New England hospitality.

About Marie Wagner

Marie Wagner says she "sort of stumbled" onto this design as she was planning a wedding gift for her daughter. An "old hand" at knitting Irish fisherman patterns—having knit "acres" of sweaters, ponchos, and baby afghans for her three children and five grandchildren—she began to experiment with a variety of stitches. The popcorn stitch resembled the "hide of a pineapple," she recalls, and in New England, where her daughter had lived for many years, the pineapple is a decorative motif associated with hospitality. Being partial to the pineapple motif herself, Marie thought this a fitting symbol for a newlyweds' bedspread.

SIZE: About 49″ × 56″, plus 8″ fringe on each side

MATERIALS: Yarn: Knitting worsted, 72 oz natural white; **knitting needles:** size 8 (5.00 mm) *or the size that gives you the correct gauge;* cable or dp needle, large crochet hook.

GAUGE: In stockinette st, 5 sts = 1″; 13 rows = 2″.

PATTERN STITCHES: Honeycomb Stitch: Worked on 40 sts. **Row 1 (right side):** K across. **Row 2 and all even-numbered rows:** P across. **Row 3:** * Sl next 2 sts to dp needle and hold in back, k 2, k 2 from dp needle (back cross made), sl next 2 sts to dp needle and hold in front, k 2, k 2 from dp needle (front cross made); repeat from * across. **Row 5:** K across. **Row 7:** * Front cross, back cross; repeat from * across. **Row 8:** P across. Repeat Rows 1 through 8 for pattern st.

Twisted Cable: Worked on 6 sts. **Row 1 (right side):** K across. **Row 2 and all even-numbered rows:** P across. **Row 3:** Sl first 3 sts to dp needle and hold in front, k 3, k 3 from dp needle. **Rows 4 through 10:** Repeat Row 2, then repeat Rows 1 and 2 three times. Repeat Rows 1 through 10 for pattern st.

Chain Cable: Worked on 12 sts. **Row 1 (right side):** P 3, k 6, p 3. **Row 2:** K 3, p 6, k 3. **Row 3:** Sl 3 sts to dp needle and hold in back, k 3, p 3 from dp needle (back p cross); sl next 3 sts to dp needle and hold in front, p 3, k 3 from dp needle (front p cross). **Row 4:** P 3, k 6, p 3. **Row 5:** K 3, p 6, k 3. **Rows 6 through 12:** Repeat Row 4, then repeat Rows 5 and 4 three times. **Row 13:** Front p cross, back p cross. **Row 14:** Repeat Row 2. Repeat Rows 1 through 14 for pattern st.

Reverse Stockinette Stitch: Row 1 (right side): P across. **Row 2:** K across. Repeat Rows 1 and 2 for pattern st.

Bobble Stitch: Worked on 5 sts. **Row 1 (right side):** K 1, p 3, k 1. **Row 2:** P 1, k 3, p 1. **Rows 3 and 4:** Repeat Rows 1 and 2. **Row 5:** K 1, p 1, make bobble as follows: (k 1, p 1, k 1, p 1, k 1) in next st; turn; k 5; turn; p 5; turn; k 5; turn; p 5 tog (bobble made); p 1, k 1. **Rows 6 through 12:** Repeat Row 2, then repeat Rows 1 and 2 three times. Repeat Rows 1 through 12 for pattern st.

Bramble Stitch: Worked on 36 sts. **Row 1 (right side):** P across. **Row 2:** * (K 1, p 1, k 1) in next st, p 3 tog: repeat from * across. **Row 3:** P across. **Row 4:** * P 3 tog, (k 1, p 1, k 1) in next st; repeat from * across. Repeat Rows 1 through 4 for pattern st.

Pineapple: (*Note:* Pattern st begins and ends with 29 sts. Number of sts on rows in between varies.) **Row 1 (right side):** P across. **Row 2:** K across. **Rows 3 through 18:** Repeat Rows 1 and 2 eight times. **Row 19:** P 12; sl next st to dp needle and hold in back, k 1, p st from dp needle (right twist made), p 1; sl next st to dp needle and hold in front, p 1, k st from dp needle (left twist made), p 12. **Row 20:** K 12, p 1, (k 1, p 1, k 1) in next st, p 1, (k 1, p 1, k 1) in next st, p 1, k 12. **Row 21:** P 11, right twist, p 7, left twist, p 11. **Row 22:** K 11, p 1, * (k 1, p 1, k 1) in next st, p 3 tog *; repeat from * to * once, (k 1, p 1, k 1) in next st, p 1, k 11. **Row 23:** P 10, right twist, p 11, left twist, p 10. **Row 24:** K 10, p 1, repeat from * to * (see Row 22) 3 times, (k 1, p 1, k 1) in next st, p 1, k 10. **Row 25:** P 9, right twist, p 15, left twist, p 9. **Row 26:** K 9, p 1, repeat from * to * (Row 22) 4 times, (k 1, p 1, k 1) in next st, p 1, k 9. **Row 27:** P 8, right twist, p 19, left twist, p 8. **Row 28:** K 8, p 1, repeat from * to * 5 times, (k 1, p 1, k 1) in next st, p 1, k 8. **Row 29:** P 7, right twist, p 23, left twist, p 7. **Row 30:** K 7, p 1; repeat from * to * 6 times, (k 1, p 1, k 1) in next st, p 1, k 7. **Row 31:** P 6, right twist, p 27, left twist, p 6. **Row 32:** K 6, p 1, repeat from * to * 7 times, (k 1, p 1, k 1) in next st, p 1, k 6. **Row 33:** P 5, right twist, p 31, left twist, p 5. **Row 34:** K 5, p 1, repeat from * to * 8 times, (k 1, p 1, k 1) in next st, p 1, k 5. **Row 35:** P 4, right twist, p 35, left twist, p 4. **Row 36:** K 4, p 1, repeat from * to * 9 times, (k 1, p 1, k 1) in next st, p 1, k 4. **Row 37:** P 4, k 1, p 39, k 1, p 4. **Row 38:** K 4, p 1, ** p 3 tog, (k 1, p 1, k 1) in next st **; repeat from ** to ** 8 times, p 3 tog, p 1, k 4. **Row 39:** P 4, k 1, p 37, k 1, p 4.

Rows 40 through 55: Repeat Rows 36 through 39 four times. **Row 56:** K 4, p 1, k 1, repeat from ** to ** (see Row 38) 8 times, p 3 tog, k 1, p 1, k 4. **Row 57:** P 4, left twist, p 33, right twist, p 4, **Row 58:** K 5, p 1, k 1, repeat from ** to ** 7 times, p 3 tog, k 1, p 1, k 5. **Row 59:** P 5, left twist, p 29, right twist, p 5. **Row 60:** K 6, p 1, k 1, repeat from ** to ** 6 times, p 3 tog, k 1, p 1, k 6. **Row 61:** P 6, left twist, p 25, right twist, p 6. **Row 62:** K 7, p 1, k 1, repeat from ** to ** 5 times, p 3 tog, k 1, p 1, k 7. **Row 63:** P 7, left twist, p 21, right twist, p 7. **Row 64:** K 8, p 1, k 1, repeat from ** to ** 4 times, p 3 tog, k 1, p 1, k 8.

Row 65: P 8, left twist, p 17, right twist, p 8. **Row 66:** K 9, p 1, k 1, repeat from ** to ** 3 times, p 3 tog, k 1, p 1, k 9. **Row 67:** P 9, left twist, p 13, right twist, p 9. **Row 68:** K 10, p 1, k 1, repeat from ** to ** twice, p 3 tog, k 1, p 1, k 10. **Row 69:** P 10, left twist, p 9, right twist, p 10. **Row 70:** K 11, p 1, k 1, repeat from ** to ** once, p 3 tog, k 1, p 1, k 11. **Row 71:** P 11, left twist, p 5, right twist, p 11. **Row 72:** K 12, p 1, k 1, p 3 tog, p 1, k 12. **Row 73:** P 12, left twist, p 1, right twist, p 12. **Row 74:** K 13, p 3, k 13. **Row 75:** P 13, k 3, p 13.

Row 76: K 13, p 3, k 13. **Row 77:** P 11, p 2 tog, k in front and back of next st (k inc made), k 1, inc, p 2 tog, p 11. **Row 78:** K 12, p 5, k 12. **Row 79:** P 10, p 2 tog, yo, k 1, yo, k 3, yo, k 1, yo, p 2 tog, p 10. (*Note:* In purl areas p in back and front of next st for p inc.) **Row 80:** K 11, p 3, inc, p 1, inc, p 3, k 11. **Row 81:** P 9, p 2 tog, (k 1, yo) twice, (k 1, p 2) twice, (k 1, yo) twice, k 1, p 2 tog, p 9. **Row 82:** K 10, p 5, k 1, inc, p 1, inc, k 1, p 5, k 10. **Row 83:** P 8, p 2 tog, k 2, yo, k 1, yo, k 2, p 3, k 1, p 3, k 2, yo, k 1, yo, k 2, p 2 tog, p 8. **Row 84:** K 9, p 7, k 1, inc, k 1, p 1, k 1, inc, k 1, p 7, k 9. **Row 85:** P 7, p 2 tog, k 3, yo, k 1, yo, (k 3, p 3) twice, k 3, yo, k 1, yo, k 3, p 2 tog, p 7. **Row 86:** K 8, p 9, k 1, inc, k 1, p 3, k 1, inc, k 1, p 9, k 8. **Row 87:** P 6, p 2 tog, k 4, yo, k 1, yo, k 4, p 4, k 3, p 4, k 4, yo, k 1, yo, k 4, p 2 tog, p 6. **Row 88:** K 7, p 11, k 1, inc, k 2, p 3, k 2, inc, k 1, p 11, k 7. **Row 89:** P 5, p 2 tog, sl 1, k 1, psso, k 7, k 2 tog, p 5, k 3, p 5, sl 1, k 1, psso, k 7, k 2 tog, p 2 tog, p 5. **Row 90:** K 6, p 9, k 5, inc, p 1, inc, k 5, p 9, k 6. **Row 91:** P 4, p 2 tog, sl 1, k 1, psso, k 5, k 2 tog, p 5, yo, k 1, yo, p 1, k 1, p 1, yo, k 1, yo, p 5, sl 1, k 1, psso, k 5, k 2 tog, p 2 tog, p 4. **Row 92:** K 5, p 7, k 5, p 3, inc, p 1, inc, p 3, k 5, p 7, k 5. **Row 93:** P 3, p 2 tog, sl 1, k 1, psso, k 3, k 2 tog, p 5, (k 1, yo) twice, (k 1, p 2) twice, (k 1, yo) twice, k 1, p 5, sl 1, k 1, psso, k 3, k 2 tog, p 2 tog, p 3. **Row 94:** K 4, p 5, k 5, p 5, k 1, inc, p 1, inc, k 1, p 5, k 5, p 5, k 4. **Row 95:** P 2, p 2 tog, sl 1, k 1, psso, k 1, k 2 tog, p 5, k 2, yo, k 1, yo, k 2, p 3, k 1, p 3, k 2, yo, k 1, yo, k 2, p 5, sl 1, k 1, psso, k 1, k 2 tog, p 2 tog, p 2. **Row 96.** K 3, p 3, k 5, p 7, k 1, inc, p 3, inc, k 1, p 7, k 5, p 3, k 3. **Row 97:** P 1, p 2 tog, k 3 tog, p 5, k 3, yo, k 1, yo, (k 3, p 3) twice, k 3, yo, k 1, yo, k 3, p 5, k 3 tog, p 2 tog, p 1.

Row 98: Repeat Row 86. **Row 99:** Repeat Row 87. **Row 100:** Repeat Row 88. **Row 101:** P 5, p 2 tog, sl 1, k 1, psso, k 7, k 2 tog, p 6, yo, k 1, yo, p 6, sl 1, k 1, psso, k 7, k 2 tog, p 2 tog, p 5. **Row 102:** K 6, p 9, k 6, p 3, k 6, p 9, k 6. **Row 103:** P 6, sl 1, k 1, psso, k 5, k 2 tog, p 6, (k 1, yo) twice, k 1, p 6, sl 1, k 1, psso, k 5, k 2 tog, p 6. **Row 104:** K 6, p 7, k 6, p 5, k 6, p 7, k 6. **Row 105:** P 6, sl 1, k 1, psso, k 3, k 2 tog, p 6, k 2, yo, k 1, yo, k 2, p 6, sl 1, k 1, psso, k 3, k 2 tog, p 6. **Row 106:** K 6, p 5, k 6, p 7, k 6, p 5, k 6. **Row 107:** P 6, sl 1, k 1, psso, k 1, k 2 tog, p 6, k 3, yo, k 1, yo, k 3, p 6, sl 1, k 1, psso, k 1, k 2 tog, p 6. **Row 108:** K 6, p 3, k 6, p 9, k 6, p 3, k 6. **Row 109:** P 6, k 3 tog, p 6, k 4, yo, k 1, yo, k 4, p 6, k 3 tog, p 6. **Row 110:** K 13, p 11, k 13. **Row 111:** P 13, sl 1, k 1, psso, k 7, k 2 tog, p 13. **Row 112:** K 13, p 9, k 13. **Row 113:** P 13, sl 1, k 1, psso, k 5, k 2 tog, p 13. **Row 114:** K 13, p 7, k 13. **Row 115:** P 13, sl 1, k 1, psso, k 3, k 2 tog, p 13. **Row 116:** K 13, p 5, k 13. **Row 117:** P 13, sl 1, k 1, psso, k 1, k 2 tog, p 13. **Row 118:** K 13, p 3, k 13. **Row 119:** P 13, k 3 tog, p 13. **Row 120:** K 12, inc, k 1, inc, k 12. Repeat Rows 1 through 120 for pattern st.

AFGHAN: Afghan consists of 7 panels knitted separately, then sewn together.

Panel A: Make 1. Starting at one end, cast on 29 sts. Work pineapple until 3 repeats have been completed, then work Rows 1 through 18 again. Bind off.

Panel B: Make 2. Starting at one end, cast on 52 sts. **Row 1 (right side);** Work Row 1 of reverse stockinette st across first 4 sts; place marker on needle; work Row 1 of twisted cable across next 6 sts; place marker on needle, reverse stockinette st on 10 sts; place marker on needle, work Row 1 of chain cable on 12 sts; place marker on needle, twisted cable on 6 sts; place marker on needle; reverse stockinette st on last 4 sts. Work in patterns as established until panel is same length as Panel A. Bind off.

Panel C: Make 2. Starting at one end, cast on 46 sts. **Row 1 (right side):** Work Row 1 of bobble st across first 5 sts; place marker; work Row 1 of bramble st across next 36 sts; place marker; bobble st on last 5 sts. Work in patterns as established until panel is same length as panel A. Bind off.

Panel D: Mark 2. Starting at one end, cast on 40 sts. Work in honeycomb st until panel is same length as Panel A. Bind off.

FINISHING: Sew panels together in sequence of D, B, C, A, C, B, and D.

FRINGE: See Fringes, page 196. For each fringe, cut seven 24" strands yarn. Make fringe every 1" all around afghan. Divide each fringe in half, forming two 7-strand bunches. Knot bunches from adjacent fringes together about 1" below first row of knots. Divide fringes in half again and knot adjacent bunches of original fringes 1" below previous knots. Trim ends to about 6".

Marriage Lines

Knit throw by Fran Weisse of Natick, Massachusetts

Traditional knitting patterns personalize a gift of heirloom quality.

About Fran Weisse

It was to be a very special occasion: Fran Weisse's brother was getting married at Longfellow's famous Wayside Inn in Sudbury, Massachusetts. It was also where Fran and her husband were married—and now they were to serve as best man and matron of honor. So Fran planned a very special wedding present: a sampler afghan that would echo elements in the newlyweds' lives. He grew up on a lake, summered at the ocean, and loves everything nautical. She is a Kansas farm girl. So Fran picked special stitch patterns: for him, *lobster cable on seaweed, scallop shells, wave stitch, anchors, clamshells, little birds*; for her, *sheaf stitch, reverse diagonal* (her son says it looks like tractor tracks), *wheat ear cable with grains of wheat, horseshoe, welted leaf,* and *lines* "Their" patterns include one called *marriage butterflies.* with initials and wedding date, *tree of life,* and *banjo cable* with garter stitch "staff', since they are both musicians.

SIZE: About 42″ × 70″, plus 5″ fringe

MATERIALS: Yarn: Knitting worsted, 50 oz off-white; **knitting needles:** 1 pair size 7 (4.50 mm) *or the size that gives you the correct gauge;* dp needle size 7.

GAUGE: 9 sts = 2″, overall average. Each block measures 14″ square.

Note: This wedding-gift afghan was worked in 15 blocks with pattern stitches chosen to represent aspects of the bride's and groom's interests. Specific pattern directions are given to duplicate this afghan, as well as basic directions to allow you to substitute your own patterns and personalize the center (marriage lines) block with the initials and date you wish.

BASIC BLOCK: Seed Stitch Pattern (Borders): Worked on uneven number of sts. **Row 1:** K 1, * p 1, k 1; repeat from * across. Repeat this row for pattern.

Block: Bottom Border: Cast on 63 sts. Work 9 rows of seed st. (*Note:* Because some patterns, such as cables, "pull in" more than others, the number of center sts worked in pattern between seed st borders will vary, and you will need to increase or decrease to the required number of sts for your pattern on next row. If you are choosing your own pattern stitch, make a practice swatch first to determine how many sts your pattern requires to measure 11″ across.) **10th row (right side):** Work seed st on first 7 sts (border), place a marker on needle, work Row 1 of desired pattern over center sts to last 7 sts, increasing or decreasing as necessary for pattern, place another marker on needle, and work last 7 sts in seed st (border). Slipping markers each row, work 7 sts at each edge in seed st and center sts between markers in pattern until block measures 12½″ from beginning. **Top Border: Next row:** Work first 7 sts in seed st, remove marker, work seed st across center sts, decreasing or increasing as necessary to obtain 49 sts to next marker, remove marker, work in seed st on last 7 sts. Work all 63 sts in seed st for 8 more rows. Bind off.

SHEAF STITCH BLOCK: Sheaf Stitch Pattern: Worked on 66 sts. **Row 1 and all right-side rows:** P 2, * k 2, p 2; repeat from * across. (*Note:* To inc on first row, work each (p 2) by p into front loop, then back loop of same st.) **Row 2:** K 2, * p 2, k 2; repeat from * across. **Row 4:** K 2, * work sheaf tie over next 6 sts as follows: yarn forward, slip next 6 sts to dp needle, wrap yarn around sts on needle front to back twice and just tightly enough to make tie ¾″ wide, then work (p 2, k 2, p 2) from dp needle (sheaf tie completed), k 2; repeat from * across. **Row 6:** Repeat Row 2. **Row 8:** K 2, p 2, k 2, * work sheaf tie on next 6 sts, k 2; repeat from * across to last 4 sts, p 2, k 2. **Row 10:** Repeat Row 2. Repeat Rows 1 through 10 for pattern.

Block: Work as for Basic Block, increasing 17 sts between markers of first row of pattern.

LOBSTER CABLE ON SEAWEED BLOCK: Lobster Cable Pattern: Worked on 16 sts. **Row 1 (right side):** P 4, k 1, p 6, k 1, p 4. **Row 2:** K 4, (p 2, k 4) twice. **Row 3:** P 4, (k 2, p 4) twice. **Rows 4 and 5:** Repeat Rows 2 and 3. **Row 6:** Repeat Row 2. **Row 7 (cable twist):** P 4, slip next 2 sts to dp needle and hold in front, p 1, p into front loop, then back loop of next st (inc made), working through back loops k 2 tog from dp needle (dec made), slip next 2 sts to dp needle and hold in back, k 2 tog, p into front, then back loop of first st on dp needle, p next st from dp needle (cable twist completed), p 4. **Row 8:** K 16. Repeat these 8 rows for pattern.

Seaweed Pattern: Worked on 18 sts. **Row 1 (right side):** (P 2, k 4) 3 times. **Row 2:** (P 4, k 2) 3 times. **Row 3:** (P 3, k 3) 3 times. **Row 4:** Repeat Row 3. **Row 5:** Repeat row 2. **Row 6:** Repeat Row 1. **Row 7:** K 1, (p 4, k 2) twice, p 4, k 1. **Row 8:** P 1, (k 4, p 2) twice, k 4, p 1. **Row 9:** K 2, (p 3, k 3) twice, p 3, k 1. **Row 10:** P 1, (k 3, p 3) twice, k 3, p 2. **Row 11:** K 3, (p 2, k 4) twice, p 2, k 1. **Row 12:** P 1, k 2, (p 4, k 2) twice, p 3. Repeat these 12 rows for pattern.

Block: Work as for Basic Block, establishing pattern on center sts between markers as follows: work lobster cable pattern on first 16 sts; work seaweed pattern, increasing 1 st on first row to work pattern on 18 sts; work lobster cable pattern on remaining 16 sts before marker.

WELTED LEAF BLOCK: Welted Leaf Pattern: Worked on 48 sts. **Row 1 (right side):** Knit. **Row 2:** Purl. **Row 3:** * K 4, p 4; repeat from * across. **Row 4:** K 3, * p 4, k 4; repeat from * across, ending last repeat with k 1. **Row 5:** P 2, * k 4, p 4; repeat from * across, ending last repeat with p 2. **Row 6:** K 1, * p 4, k 4; repeat from * across, ending last repeat with k 3. **Rows 7 through 9:** Repeat Rows 4 through 6. **Row 10:** * P 4, k 4; repeat from * across. **Row 11:** Knit. **Rows 12 and 13:** Purl. **Row 14:** Knit. **Rows 15 through 42:** Repeat Rows 1 through 14 twice. **Row 43:** Repeat Row 3. **Row 44:** P 1, * k 4, p 4; repeat from * across, ending last repeat with p 3. **Row 45:** K 2, * p 4, k 4; repeat from * across, ending last repeat with k 2. **Row 46:** P 3, * k 4, p 4; repeat from * across, ending last repeat with p 1. **Rows 47 through 49:** Repeat Rows 44 through 46. **Row 50:** Repeat Row 10. **Row 51:** Purl. **Rows 52 and 53:** Knit. **Row 54 and 55:** Purl. **Row 56:** Knit. **Rows 57 through 84:** Repeat Rows 43 through 56 twice (pattern completed).

Block: Work as for Basic Block, decreasing 1 st between markers on first row of pattern.

BANJO CABLE BLOCK: Banjo Cable Pattern: Worked on 12 sts. **Row 1 (right side):** P 4, k 4, p 4. **Row 2:** K 4, p 4, k 4. **Row 3 (outward twist):** P 2, slip next 3 sts to dp needle and hold in back, k 1, work (p 1, k 1, p 1) from dp needle, slip next st to dp needle and hold in front of work, k 1, p 1, k 1, then k 1 from dp needle, p 2. **Row 4:** K 2, p 1, (k 1, p 1) 3 times, p 1, k 2. **Row 5:** P 2, k 1, (p 1, k 1) 3 times, k 1, p 2. **Rows 6 through 9:** Repeat rows 4 and 5 twice more. **Row 10:** Repeat Row 4. **Row 11 (inward twist):** P 2, slip next st to dp needle and hold in front, p 2, k 1, then k 1 from dp needle, slip next 3 sts to dp needle and hold in back, k 1, work (k 1, p 2) from dp needle, p 2. **Row 12:** Repeat Row 2. **Rows 13 through 16:** Repeat Rows 1 and 2 twice more. Repeat these 16 rows for pattern.

Ridged Pattern: Worked on 8 or 12 sts. **Row 1 (right side):** Knit. **Row 2:** Purl. **Rows 3 through 6:** Repeat Rows 1 and 2 twice. **Rows 7 through 15:** Knit. **Row 16:** Purl. Repeat these 16 rows for pattern.

Block: Work as for Basic Block, establishing patterns on center sts between markers as follows: work ridged pattern, increasing 1 st on first row to work pattern on 8 sts; work banjo cable pattern on next 12 sts, ridged pattern on next 12 sts, banjo cable on next 12 sts, ridged pattern (increasing 1 st on first row to work pattern on remaining 8 sts before marker).

BUTTERFLIES BLOCK: Butterflies Pattern: Worked on 49 sts. **Row 1 (right side):** K 2, * with yarn in front of work slip next 5 sts as if to p, k 5 (strand lies across work in front of slipped sts); repeat from * across, ending last

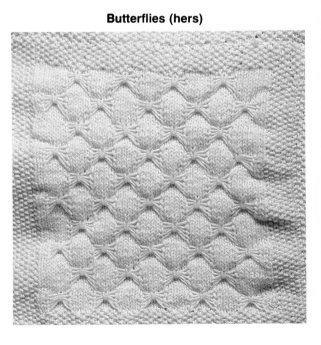

Butterflies (hers)

repeat with k 2. **Row 2:** Purl. **Rows 3 through 8:** Repeat Rows 1 and 2 three times more. **Row 9:** Repeat Row 1. **Row 10:** P 4, * with tip of right needle pick up 5 strands at front of work and place on left needle, p strands tog with next st, p 9; repeat from * across, ending last repeat with p 4. **Row 11:** K 7, * with yarn in front slip next 5 sts as if to p, k 5; repeat from * across, ending last repeat with k 7. **Row 12:** Purl. **Rows 13 through 18:** Repeat Rows 11 and 12 three times more. **Row 19:** Repeat Row 11. **Row 20:** P 9; * p next st, catching 5 strands in st, then p 9; repeat from * across. Repeat these 20 rows for pattern.

Block: Work same as for Basic Block.

TREE OF LIFE BLOCK: Right Border Pattern: Worked on 13 sts. **Row 1 (right side):** K 2, p 2, k 4, p 2, k 3. **Row 2:** P 3, k 2, p 4, k 2, p 2. **Rows 3 and 4:** Repeat Rows 1 and 2. **Row 5:** K 1, (p 4, k 2) twice. **Row 6:** (P 2, k 4) twice, p 1. **Rows 7 and 8:** Repeat Rows 5 and 6. Repeat these 8 rows for pattern.

Tree of Life Pattern: Worked on 23 sts. **Row 1 (right side):** P 1, k 9, p 1, k 1, p 1, k 9, p 1. **Row 2:** K 1, p 8, k 1, (p 1, k 1) twice, p 8, k 1. **Row 3:** P 1, k 7, p 1, k 5, p 1, k 7, p 1. **Row 4:** K 1, p 6, (k 1, p 3) twice, k 1, p 6, k 1. **Row 5:** P 1, k 5, p 1, k 9, p 1, k 5, p 1. **Row 6:** K 1, p 4, k 1, (p 5, k 1) twice, p 4, k 1. **Row 7:** P 1, k 3, p 1, k 13, p 1, k 3, p 1. **Row 8:** K 1, p 2, (k 1, p 7) twice, k 1, p 2, k 1. **Row 9:** P 1, k 1, p 1, k 17, p 1, k 1, p 1. **Row 10:** K 1, (p 10, k 1) twice. Repeat these 10 rows for pattern.

Left Border Pattern: Worked on 13 sts. **Row 1 (right side):** K 3, p 2, k 4, p 2, k 2. **Row 2:** P 2, k 2, p 4, k 2, p 3. **Rows 3 and 4:** Repeat Rows 1 and 2. **Row 5:** (K 2, p 4) twice, k 1. **Row 6:** P 1, (k 4, p 2) twice. **Rows 7 and 8:** Repeat Rows 5 and 6. Repeat these 8 rows for pattern.

Block: Work as for Basic Block, establishing patterns on center sts between markers as follows: right border pattern on first 13 sts, tree of life pattern on next 23 sts, and left border pattern on last 13 sts before marker.

SCALLOPS BLOCK: Scallops Pattern: Worked on 49 sts. **Row 1 (right side):** K 1, * yo (inc made), k 1, (p 1, k 1) 7 times, yo (another inc made), k 1; repeat from * twice more (6 inc). **Row 2:** K 2, * p 1, (k 1, p 1) 7 times, k 3; repeat from * across, ending last repeat with k 2. **Row 3:** K 2, * yo, k 1, (p 1, k 1) 7 times, yo, k 3; repeat from * across, ending last repeat with k 2 (6 inc). **Row 4:** K 3, *

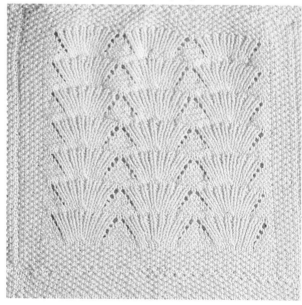

Scallops (his)

p 1, (k 1, p 1) 7 times, k 5; repeat from * across, ending with k 3. **Row 5:** K 3, * yo, k 1, (p 1, k 1) 7 times, yo, k 5; repeat from * across, ending last repeat with k 3 (6 inc). **Row 6:** K 4, * p 1, (k 1, p 1) 7 times, k 7; repeat from * ending with k 4. **Row 7:** K 4, * yo, k 1, (p 1, k 1) 7 times, yo, k 7; repeat from * across, ending last repeat with k 4 (6 inc—73 sts). **Row 8:** K 5, p 1, (k 1, p 1) 7 times, k 9; repeat from *, ending with k 5. **Row 9:** K 5, * (sl 1, k 1, psso) 3 times, sl 1, k 2 tog, psso, (k 2 tog) 3 times, k 9; repeat from * across, ending last repeat with k 5 (49 sts). **Row 10:** Purl. Repeat these 10 rows for pattern.

Block: Work same as for Basic Block. *Note:* When assembling afghan use cast-on edge as top edge of block.

MARRIAGE LINES BLOCK: You can personalize this block by charting out desired initials and date following the directions below, or leave blank and simply work the zigzag pattern.

Initials and Date: To chart each letter or number, mark off on graph paper a rectangle 11 squares high by 6 squares wide. For date, use number(s) for month (1 for Jan, 12 for Dec) and 4 numbers for year. Use 3 initials for each of 2 people, or repeat same initials on each side of block. Plot out desired letter or number on graph with edges of figure filling out chart to edges of rectangle. Each square of chart equals 1 stitch. To knit letters and numbers, work background sts in stockinette st and figure sts in garter st so that horizontal lines are formed by garter st ridge and vertical lines resemble seed st.

Zigzag Pattern: Worked on 22 sts. **Row 1 (right side:** P 1, k 5, p 1, (k 2, p 1) 3 times, k 5, p 1. **Row 2:** P 5, k 1, (p 2, k 1) 3 times, p 7. **Row 3:** P 1, k 7, p 1, (k 2, p 1) 3 times, k 3, p 1. **Row 4:** P 3, k 1, (p 2, k 1) 3 times, p 9. **Row 5:** Repeat Row 3. **Row 6:** Repeat Row 2. **Row 7:** Repeat Row 1. **Row 8:** P 7, k 1, (p 2, k 1) 3 times, p 5. **Row 9:** P 1, k 3, p 1, (k 2, p 1) 3 times, k 7, p 1. **Row 10:** P 9, k 1, (p 2, k 1) 3 times, p 3. **Row 11:** Repeat Row 9. **Row 12:** Repeat Row 8. Repeat these 12 rows for pattern.

Block: To work Zigzag Pattern without initials or date, work as for Basic Block, establishing pattern on center sts between markers as follows: work stockinette st on first 14 sts, work zigzag pattern, increasing 1 st to work pattern on 22 sts, work stockinette st on last 14 sts before marker.

185

To work initials and date, work as for Basic Block until bottom border is completed. **Row 10:** Work 7 sts in seed st, marker; k across, increasing 1 st to work 50 sts, marker; work last 7 sts in seed st. Keeping 7 sts at each edge in seed st, work center 50 sts between markers as follows: **Next (11th) Row:** Purl. **Row 12 (right side):** Establish date, starting with last numeral of year (for instance, the "4" used in the 1984 date on original afghan), as follows: k 1, work last numeral of year on next 6 sts, (k 2, next numeral on next 6 sts) 3 times, k 4, work 2nd numeral of month on 6 sts (if month has only one numeral, k these 6 sts), k 2, work first numeral of month on 6 sts, k 1. Complete charts for date, ending right-side row. **Next row:** Purl. **Establish Zigzag Pattern:** Work stockinette st on first 14 sts, work zigzag pattern on center 22 sts, work stockinette st on last 14 sts. Work as established until 8th row of zigzag pattern is completed. **Establish Initials: Next row (right side):** K 4, work last initial on next 6 sts, k 4; continue zigzag pattern on center 22 sts; k 4, work other last initial on 6 sts, k 4. Work as established, keeping center 22 sts in zigzag pattern throughout and completing chart for last initial. Then work 5 rows in stockinette st; work chart for middle initial directly above last initial. Then work 5 rows stockinette st; work chart for first initial directly above middle initial. When first initial chart is completed, discontinue patterns and work stockinette st on 50 sts for 7 more rows, decreasing 1 st in center of block on last row. Remove markers and work seed st on all 63 sts for 9 rows. Bind off.

HORSESHOE BLOCK: Horseshoe Pattern: Worked on 51 sts. **Row 1 (right side):** K 1, * yo, k 3, sl 1, k 2 tog, psso, k 3, yo, k 1; repeat from * 4 times more (51 sts). **Row 2:** Purl. **Row 3:** P 1, * k 1, yo, k 2, sl 1, k 2 tog, psso, k 2, yo, k 1, p 1; repeat from * 4 times more. **Row 4:** K 1, p to last st, k 1. **Row 5:** P 1, * k 2, yo, k 1, sl 1, k 2 tog, psso, k 1, yo, k 2, p 1; repeat from * 4 times more. **Row 6:** Repeat Row 4. **Row 7:** P 1, * k 3, yo, sl 1, k 2 tog, psso, yo, k 3, p 1; repeat from * across. **Row 8:** Repeat Row 4. Repeat these 8 rows for pattern.

Block: Work as for Basic Block, increasing 2 sts between markers on first row of pattern.

ANCHORS BLOCK: Anchors Pattern: Worked on 50 sts. **Row 1 (right side):** Knit. **Row 2:** P 2, * k 2, p 17, k 2 *, p

4, repeat * to * once more, p 2. Repeat these 2 rows 4 times more. **Row 11:** Knit. **Row 12:** P 2, * k 2, p 8, k 1, p 8, k 2 *, p 4, repeat * to * once, p 2. **Rows 13 and 14:** Repeat Rows 11 and 12. **Row 15:** K 11, p 3, k 22, p 3, k 11. **Row 16:** P 2, * k 2, p 6, k 5, p 6, k 2 *, p 4, repeat * to * once, p 2. **Row 17:** K 9, p 2, k 3, p 2, k 18, p 2, k 3, p 2, k 9. **Row 18:** P 2, * k 2, p 4, k 2, p 2, k 1, p 2, k 2, p 4, k 2 *, p 4, repeat * to * once, p 2. **Row 19:** K 7, p 2, k 7, p 2, k 14, p 2, k 7, p 2, k 7. **Row 20:** P 2, * k 2, p 2, k 2, p 4, k 1, p 4, k 2, p 2, k 2 *, p 4, repeat * to * once, p 2. **Row 21:** K 6, p 3, k 4, p 1, k 2, p 3, k 12, p 3, k 4, p 1, k 2, p 3, k 6. **Row 22:** P 2, * k 2, p 3, k 1, p 2, k 1, p 1, k 1, p 4, k 1, p 3, k 2 *, p 4, repeat * to * once, p 2. **Row 23:** K 15, p 1, k 24, p 1, k 9. **Row 24:** P 2, * k 2, p 6, k 1, p 1, k 1, p 8, k 2 *, p 4, repeat * to * once, p 2. **Row 25:** K 13, p 1, k 24, p 1, k 11. **Row 26:** P 2, * k 2, p 8, k 1, p 8, k 2 *, p 4, repeat * to * once, p 2. **Row 27.** K 11, p 1, k 24, p 1, k 13. **Row 28:** P 2, * k 2, p 8, k 1, p 1, k 1, p 6, k 2 *, p 4, repeat * to * once, p 2. **Row 29:** K 9, p 1, k 24, p 1, k 15. **Row 30:** Repeat Row 28. **Row 31:** Repeat Row 27. **Row 32:** P 2, * k 2, p 4, k 9, p 4, k 2 *, p 4, repeat * to * once, p 2. **Row 33:** K 9, p 7, k 18, p 7, k 9. **Row 34:** Repeat Row 12. **Row 35:** K 11, p 1, k 1, p 1, k 22, p 1, k 1, p 1, k 11. **Row 36:** Repeat Row 12. **Rows 37 through 72:** Repeat Rows 11 through 36 once more. **Rows 73 through 82:** Repeat Rows 1 and 2 five times more. This completes pattern.

Block: Work as for Basic Block, increasing 1 st between markers on first row of pattern.

TRACTOR TRACKS BLOCK: Tractor Tracks Pattern: Worked on 48 sts. **Row 1 (right side):** * K 5, p 1, k 1, p 1; repeat from * across. **Row 2:** * K 1, p 1, k 1, p 5; repeat from * across. **Row 3:** * K 1, p 5, k 1, p 1; repeat from * across. **Row 4:** * K 1, p 1, k 5, p 1; repeat from * across. **Row 5:** Repeat Row 4. **Row 6:** Repeat Row 3. **Row 7:** Repeat Row 2. **Row 8:** Repeat Row 1. **Row 9:** (K 1, p 1) twice, * k 5, p 1, k 1, p 1; repeat from * across, ending with k 4. **Row 10:** P 4, * k 1, p 1, k 1, p 5; repeat from * across, ending with p 1. **Row 11:** P 2, * k 1, p 1, k 1, p 5; repeat from * across, ending with p 3. **Row 12:** K 3, * p 1, k 1, p 1, k 5; repeat from * across, ending with k 2. **Row 13:** K 3, * p 1, k 1, p 1, k 5; repeat from * across, ending with k 2. **Row 14:** Repeat Row 11. **Row 15:** Repeat Row 10. **Row 16:** Repeat Row 9. Repeat these 16 rows for pattern.

Block: Work as for Basic Block, decreasing 1 st between markers on first row of pattern.

WHEAT BLOCK: Grains of Wheat Pattern: Worked on 20 sts. **Row 1 (right side):** K 1, * p 2, skip next st and k through back loop of 2nd st on left needle, leave on needle, k skipped st, drop both sts from needle (left twist made on 2 sts); repeat from * 3 times more, p 2, k 1. **Row 2:** K 3, (p 2, k 2) 3 times, p 2, k 3. **Row 3:** K 3, * skip next st and k through front loop of 2nd st on left needle, leave on needle, k skipped st, drop both sts from needle (right twist made on 2 sts), k 2; repeat from * 4 times, k last st. **Row 4:** Purl. **Row 5:** K 1, (work left twist as for Row 1, p 2) 4 times, left twist, k 1. **Row 6:** K 1, (p 2, k 2) 4 times, p 2, k 1. **Row 7:** K 1, (work right twist as for Row 3, k 2) 4 times, right twist, k 1. **Row 8:** Purl. Repeat these 8 rows for pattern.

Wheat Ear Cable: Worked on 17 sts. **Row 1 (right side):** P 2, k 13, p 2. **Row 2 and all wrong-side rows:** K 2, p 13, k 2. **Row 3 (cable twist row):** P 2, slip next 3 sts to dp needle and hold in front, k 3, k 3 from dp needle, k 1, slip next 3 sts to dp needle and hold in back, k 3, k 3 from dp needle, p 2. **Row 5:** Repeat Row 1. **Row 6:** Repeat Row 2. Repeat these 6 rows for pattern.

Block: Work as for Basic Block, establishing patterns on center sts between markers as follows: work grains of wheat pattern and inc 2 sts on first row to work on 20 sts, work wheat ear cable and inc 4 sts on first row to work on 17 sts, work grains of wheat pattern and inc 2 sts on first row to work on last 20 sts before marker. *Note:* On original afghan, cast-on edge was used as top of block.

WAVES BLOCK: Waves Pattern: Worked on 49 sts. **Row 1 (right side):** P 1, (k 7, p 1) 6 times. **Row 2:** K 2, (p 5, k 3) 5 times, p 5, k 2. **Row 3:** P 3, (k 3, p 5) 5 times, k 3, p 3. **Row 4:** K 4, (p 1, k 7) 5 times, p 1, k 4. **Row 5:** K 1, (p 7, k 1) 6 times. **Row 6:** P 2, (k 5, p 3) 5 times, k 5, p 2. **Row 7:** K 3, (p 3, k 5) 5 times, p 3, k 3. **Row 8:** P 4, (k 1, p 7) 5 times, k 1, p 4. Repeat these 8 rows for pattern.

Block: Work as for Basic Block. *Note:* On original afghan, cast-on edge was used as top edge of block.

LITTLE BIRDS BLOCK: Little Birds Pattern: Worked on 50 sts. **Row 1 (right side):** Knit. **Row 2:** Purl. **Rows 3 and 4:** Repeat Rows 1 and 2. **Row 5:** K 10, * sl 2 with yarn in back, k 12; repeat from * once more, sl 2 with yarn in back, k 10. **Row 6:** P 10, * sl 2 with yarn forward, p 12; repeat from * once more, sl 2 with yarn forward, p 10. **Row 7:** K 8, * sl 2 sts to dp needle and hold in back, k 1, k 2 from dp needle, sl 1 to dp needle and hold in front, k 2, k 1 from dp needle ("little bird" worked on 6 sts), k 8; repeat from * twice more. **Row 8:** Purl. **Rows 9 and 10:** Repeat Rows 1 and 2. **Row 11:** K 3, (sl 2, k 12) 3 times, sl 2, k 3. **Row 12:** P 3, (sl 2, p 12) 3 times, sl 2, p 3. **Row 13:** K 1, * work little bird on next 6 sts, k 8; repeat from * twice more, work little bird on next 6 sts, k 1. **Row 14:** Purl. Repeat Rows 3 through 14 for pattern.

Block: Work as for Basic Block, increasing 1 st between markers on first row of pattern.

CLAMSHELLS BLOCK: Clamshell Pattern: Worked on 45 sts. **Row 1 (right side):** P 2, * in next st k into front loop, back loop, front loop, back loop, and front loop (5 sts made in 1 st for clamshell), p 3; repeat from * across, ending last repeat with p 2 (89 sts on needle). **Row 2:** K 2, (p 5, k 3) 10 times, p 5, k 2. **Row 3:** P 2, (k 5 tog through back loops, p 3) 10 times, k 5 tog through back loops, p 2 (45 sts). **Row 4:** Knit. **Row 5:** P 4, (work clamshell in next st, p 3) 10 times, p in last st (85 sts). **Row 6:** K 4, (p 5, k 3) 9 times, p 5, k 4. **Row 7:** P 4, (k 5 tog through back loops, p 3) 10 times, p in last st (45 sts). **Row 8:** Knit. Repeat these 8 rows for pattern.

Block: Work same as Basic Block, decreasing 4 sts on first row of pattern.

ASSEMBLY: With yarn, sew blocks together into 3 vertical strips of 5 blocks each as follows: **Left Strip:** Starting from top, join Sheaf Stitch, Lobster Cable on Seaweed, Welted Leaf, Banjo Cable, and Butterflies Blocks. **Middle Strip:** From top, join Tree of Life, Scallops, Marriage Lines, Horseshoe, and Anchors Blocks. **Right Strip:** From top, join Tractor Tracks, Wheat, Waves, Little Birds, and Clamshells Blocks. Join strips along side edges.

FRINGE: See Fringes, page 196. For each fringe, cut 5 strands 10" long. Make fringe every 1" along ends of afghan. Trim fringe evenly.

General Directions

Crochet

HOOKS: Crochet hooks come in a wide range of sizes and lengths and are made of various materials. Steel crochet hooks are generally used for cotton thread and come in sizes 00, the largest, through 16, the smallest. Aluminum and plastic hooks, used for wool yarn and cotton thread, usually come in sizes A through K, size A being the smallest. Afghan hooks are manufactured especially for afghan stitch. They are about the length of knitting needles, 9", 10" or 14" long, and come in the same sizes as other crochet hooks.

The hook size specified in the directions for each afghan is the size most crocheters need to work specified yarn to get the correct gauge. Use the hook size *you* need to get the correct gauge (see Gauge, below).

YARNS: With a few exceptions, most of the afghans in this book are made of knitting worsted yarn. (See individual directions for specified yarns.) Whether you buy yarn or use scraps, be sure to use only all wool or all synthetic yarns in any one afghan, for ease in care of completed afghan. Buy all the yarns you will need at one time, to be sure of having the same dye lot. Slight variations in weight and color can ruin the appearance of your work.

GAUGE: It is important that you crochet to the gauge specified, so that your finished article will be the correct size. Gauge means the number of stitches and rows that make a 1" square. Make a practice piece at least 2" square, using the hook and materials specified in the directions. With a ruler, measure the number of stitches you have to 1" in your test piece.

If your stitches do not correspond to the gauge given, experiment with a different-size hook. If you have more stitches than specified to the inch, use a larger hook; if you have less, use a smaller hook. Keep changing the hook size until your gauge is the same as that specified.

Abbreviations and Terms

beg	beginning
ch	chain
dc	double crochet
dec	decrease
hdc	half double crochet
inc	increase
rnd	round
sc	single crochet
sl	slip
sl st	slip stitch
sp	space, spaces
st	stitch
sts	stitches
tog	together
tr	treble
yo	yarn over

* Repeat the instructions following the asterisk as many times as specified, in addition to the first time.

Multiple of stitches   A pattern often requires an exact number of stitches to be worked correctly. When directions say "multiple of," it means the number of stitches must be divisible by this number. For example: (Multiple of 6) would be 12, 18, 24, etc.; (multiple of 6 plus 3) would be 15, 21, 27, etc.

( )   Repeat instructions in parentheses as many times as specified. For example: "(Ch 5, sc in next sc) 5 times" means to do all that is specified in the parentheses a total of 5 times.

TO BEGIN CROCHET:

As a general rule, make a practice piece of each new stitch, working until you can do it well and comfortably.

The first loop

1. Make a loop at the end of the thread and hold loop in place with thumb and forefinger of left hand. At left is short end of thread; at right is the long or working yarn.

2. With right hand, grasp the crochet hook as you would a pencil and put hook through loop, catch working yarn and draw it through.

3. Pull short end and working yarn in opposite directions to bring loop close around the end of hook.

To hold thread

1. Measure down working yarn about 4″ from loop on hook.
2. At this point, insert yarn between ring finger and little finger of left hand.
3. Weave yarn toward back as shown: under little and ring fingers, over middle finger, and under forefinger toward you.

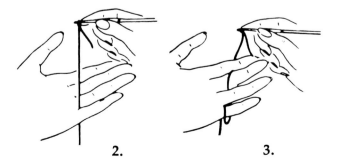

2.   **3.**

4. Grasp hook and loop with thumb and forefinger of left hand.
5. Gently pull working yarn so that it is taut but not tight.

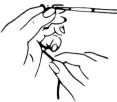

To hold hook

1. Hold hook as you would a pencil, except extend middle finger to rest near tip of hook.

2. To begin working, adjust fingers of left hand as in diagram. The middle finger is bent so it can control the tension, while the ring and little fingers prevent the yarn from moving too freely. As you practice, you will become accustomed to the correct tension. Now you are ready to begin the chain stitch.

CHAIN STITCH (ch)

1. Pass hook under yarn and catch yarn with hook. This is called yarn over (yo).

2. Draw yarn through loop on hook. This makes one chain.

3. Repeat steps 1 and 2 until you have as many chain stitches as you need. One loop always remains on hook. Keep thumb and forefinger   **191**

of your left hand near stitch on which you are working. Practice until chains are uniform.

SINGLE CROCHET (sc)

Make a foundation chain of 20 stitches for practice piece.

1. Insert hook from the front under 2 top strands of 2nd chain from hook.

2. Yarn over hook.

3. Draw through stitch. Two loops now on hook.

4. Yarn over (*below left*). Draw through 2 loops on hook. One loop remains on hook. One single crochet completed (*below right*).

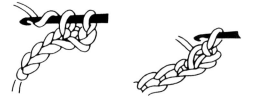

5. For next single crochet, insert hook under 2 top strands of next stitch. Repeat steps 2, 3, and 4. Make a single crochet in each chain.

6. At end of row, chain 1 (turning chain).

7. Turn work so reverse side is facing you.

8. Insert hook under 2 top strands of first single crochet. Repeat steps 2, 3, 4, 5, 6, and 7. Continue working single crochet in this manner until work is uniform and you feel familiar with the stitch. On last row, do not make a turning chain. Instead, clip yarn about 3" from work, bring loose end through the one remaining loop on hook, and pull tight. This is referred to as fastening off. You have just completed your practice piece of single crochet.

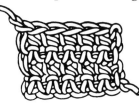

Note: In all crochet, pick up the 2 top strands of every stitch unless otherwise specified. When only one strand is picked up, the effect is different.

DOUBLE CROCHET (dc)

Make a foundation chain of 20 stitches for practice piece.

1. Yarn over, insert hook under the 2 top strands of 4th chain from hook.

2. Yarn over, draw through stitch. There are now 3 loops on hook.

3. Yarn over (*see diagram*). Draw through 2 loops. Two loops remain on hook.

4. Yarn over again. Draw through the 2 remaining loops. One loop remains on hook. One double crochet now is completed.

5. For next double crochet, yarn over, insert hook under the 2 top strands of next stitch, and repeat steps 2, 3, and 4. Repeat until you have made a double crochet in each stitch.
6. At end of row, chain 3 and turn work.

7. On next row, yarn over, skip first double crochet (ch 3 counts as first stitch), insert hook under the 2 top strands of 2nd double crochet. Repeat steps 2, 3, 4, 5, 6, and 7. *Note*: Work in top ch of turning ch 3 to make last stitch on each row.

8. Continue working double crochet in this manner until work is uniform and you feel familiar with the stitch. On last row, do not make a turning chain. Instead, clip yarn about 3″ from work, bring loose end through the one remaining loop on hook, and pull tight.

HALF DOUBLE CROCHET (hdc)

To make half double crochet, repeat steps 1 and 2 under Double Crochet but insert hook in 3rd chain from hook. At this point there are 3 loops on hook. Then yarn over and draw through all 3 loops at once. Half double crochet is now completed. At end of row, chain 2 to turn.

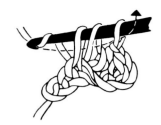

TREBLE CROCHET (tr)

Make a foundation chain of 20 stitches for practice piece.
1. Yarn over twice, insert hook under 2 top strands of 5th chain from hook.

2. Yarn over and draw a loop through the chain. There are now 4 loops on hook.
3. Yarn over again (*next diagram*). Draw through 2 loops on hook (3 loops remain on hook).

4. Yarn over again (*next diagram*). Draw through 2 loops (2 loops remain on hook).

5. Yarn over again. Draw through 2 remaining loops (1 loop remains on hook). One treble crochet is now completed. At end of row, chain 4 to turn. Continue making treble crochet in this manner until you are familiar with the stitch. Finish piece same as other pieces.   **193**

BASIC TECHNIQUES

To turn work

You will notice that stitches vary in length. Each uses a different number of chain stitches to turn at the end of a row. Below is a table showing the number of chain stitches required to make a turn for each stitch.

Single crochet (sc): ch 1
Half double crochet (hdc): ch 2
Double crochet (dc): ch 3
Treble crochet (tr): ch 4

To decrease (dec) single crochet

1. Work 1 single crochet to point where 2 loops are on hook. Draw up a loop in next stitch.

2. Yarn over, draw yarn through 3 loops at one time. One decrease made.

To decrease (dec) double crochet

1. Work 1 double crochet to point where 2 loops are on hook. Begin another double crochet in next stitch and work until 4 loops are on hook.

2. Yarn over, draw through 2 loops.

3. Yarn over, draw through 3 loops (*see diagram*). One decrease made.

To increase (inc)

When directions call for an increase, work 2 stitches in one stitch. This forms one extra stitch.

SLIP STITCH (sl st)

Make a foundation chain of 20 stitches for practice piece. Insert hook under top strand of 2nd chain from hook, yarn over. With one motion draw through stitch and loop on hook. Insert hook under top strand of next chain, then yarn over and draw through stitch and loop on hook. Repeat until you have made a slip stitch in each chain.

Slip stitch for joining

When directions say "join," always use a slip stitch.
1. Insert hook through the 2 top strands of stitch.

2. Yarn over and with one motion draw through stitch and loop on hook.

Working around the post

The "post" or "bar" is the vertical or upright portion of a stitch. When directions say to make a stitch around the post or bar of a stitch in a previous row, insert the hook *around* stitch instead of in top of stitch. See diagram below for placement of hook.

194

PLAIN AFGHAN STITCH

1. Crochet a foundation chain with 1 ch more than desired number of afghan stitches. For instance, if you wish to work 25 afghan sts, make foundation chain of 26 ch.

2. (**Row 1,** first step) Skip first ch, * insert hook into next ch and draw up a loop; repeat from * across, keeping all loops on hook.

3. (2nd step) Yo and draw through first loop on hook, * yo and draw through next 2 loops on hook; repeat from * across, working off all loops but one. This last loop is first vertical bar of next row. Do not count this first vertical bar as a st, but count each remaining bar as a st.

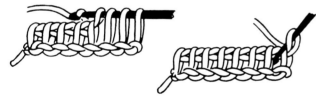

4. (**Row 2,** first step) Skip first vertical bar, * insert hook right to left under next vertical bar and draw up a loop; repeat from * across.

5. (2nd step) Work off loops same as for 2nd half of Row 1.

Repeat Row 2 for desired length.

6. On last row of work, make a slip stitch in each vertical bar to keep edge from curling.

CROSS-STITCH OVER AFGHAN STITCH

Afghan stitch forms almost perfectly square stitches. When afghan (or afghan section) is completed, embroider 1 cross-stitch over each afghan stitch, following chart for design.

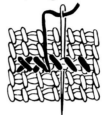

CROSS-STITCH OVER SC

To prevent distortion of design, carefully maintain specified gauge to produce square stitches. When afghan (or afghan section) is completed, embroider 1 cross-stitch over each sc stitch, following specific chart for design.

BASIC SHELL STITCH

This is the first and simplest of the many varieties of shell stitch. Once you have learned this basic stitch, you'll find directions for the others easy to follow. Make a foundation chain (multiple of 6 stitches plus 4) for practice piece. **1st row:** Work 2 dc in 4th ch from hook (half shell), skip 2 ch, sc in next ch, * skip 2 ch, 5 dc in next ch (shell made), skip 2 ch, sc in next ch. Repeat from * across, ending with 3 dc in last ch (another half shell). Ch 1, turn. **2nd row:** Sc in first dc, * skip 2 dc, shell (5 dc) in next sc, skip 2 dc, sc in center dc of next shell. Repeat from * across, ending with sc in top of half shell. Ch 3, turn. **3rd row:** Work 2 dc in first sc, * sc in center dc of next shell, shell in next sc. Repeat from * across, ending with 3 dc in last sc. Ch 1, turn. Repeat 2nd and 3rd rows for desired length.

FINISHING: After you have completed an article, thread each loose end of yarn in a needle and darn it through a solid part of the crochet to fasten it securely. Cut off remaining thread close to the work. Be sure starting ends are long enough to be fastened off.

LAUNDERING: If your work has become soiled, wash it by hand before blocking. Launder in cold-water soap or mild soap and lukewarm water. Squeeze but do not wring the article. Rinse in lukewarm water several times until soap is thoroughly removed. Roll in a bath towel to absorb some of the moisture.

BLOCKING: If an article is made up of several pieces, block them before sewing them together. If you have laundered your work, block it while still damp. If work has not been laundered, dampen by rolling up in large damp towel overnight. Place dampened work on a flat, padded surface. Gently stretch and shape it to the desired measurements: pin to surface, using rustproof pins, preferably ballpoint. Let dry thoroughly before unpinning.

(*Note:* Do not use an iron for blocking, especially on synthetic yarns, which can melt.)

SEWING: Pin together edges to be sewn, matching any pattern in rows or stitches. Thread needle with matching yarn. To begin sewing, do not knot yarn but take several over and over stitches, darning them, if possible, through a solid part of the crochet. Sew edges with a whipstitch, placing it at the edges of the work.

FRINGES: Cut yarn strands and fold strands in half. Insert crochet hook through edge of afghan from wrong side and catch strands at fold. Draw loop through. With hook, draw strand ends through loop. Pull ends to tighten knot. When all fringes are completed along edge of afghan, trim ends to an even length.

TASSELS: For each tassel, cut desired number of strands to length that is 1" longer than twice the desired finished tassel length. (For instance, for a 12"-long tassel, cut 25"-long strands.) With a separate 6" strand of yarn, tie tassel strands together at center. Fold strands in half so ends hang down with tie at center top fold. Wrap another 25" strand of yarn tightly around all strands below top fold and tie securely, leaving tie ends hanging with tassel ends. Trim tassel ends to desired length.

Knitting

NEEDLES: Knitting needles come in a wide range of sizes, types, and lengths and are made of several different materials. Straight needles with single points are used when you work back and forth in rows. Circular needles are usually used when you work in rounds. They are also used when a straight needle is not long enough to hold a large number of stitches. Double-pointed needles come in sets of four. They are used for tubular garments, when you work in rounds, or for turning cables. Large needles are used for heavy yarn and smaller needles for thinner yarn.

YARNS AND THREADS: Many types of yarn and thread are used for knitting. They differ as to twist, size, texture, and weight. The material specified in directions has always been chosen to suit the article that is being made. Only an expert knitter should attempt to substitute materials. Most of the afghans in this book are made with knitting worsted yarn, which is readily available at yarn stores or from mail-order suppliers. Whether you buy yarn or use scraps, be sure to use only all wool or all synthetic yarns in any one afghan, for ease in care of completed afghan. Buy all the thread or yarn you need at one time, to be sure of having the same dye lot. Slight variations in weight and color can ruin the appearance of your work.

GAUGE: It is most important that you knit to the gauge specified, so that your finished article will be the correct size. Gauge means the number of stitches that equal 1″ and the number of rows that equal 1″. Make a practice piece at least 4″ square, using the needles and yarn specified in the directions. With a ruler, measure the number of stitches you have to 1″ in both directions. If your stitches do not correspond to the gauge given, experiment with needles of a different size. If you have more stitches than specified to the inch, you should use larger needles. If you have less, use smaller needles. Keep changing the needle size until your gauge is exactly the same as that specified.

ABBREVIATIONS AND TERMS

beg .... beginning
dec .... decrease
dp .... double-pointed
inc.. increase
k ....knit
p .... purl
psso .... pass slipped stitch over
rnd .... round
sl.. slip
sl st....................................... slip stitch
st ....stitch
sts .... stitches
tog.. together
yb... yarn back
yf .... yarn forward
yo... yarn over

* Repeat the instructions following the asterisk as many times as specified, in addition to the first time.

Even When directions say "work even," this means to continue working without increasing or decreasing, always keeping the pattern as it has been established.

Multiple of stitches A pattern often requires an exact number of stitches to be worked correctly. When directions say "multiple of," it means the number of stitches must be divisible by this number. For example: (Multiple of 6) would be 12, 18, 24, etc.; (multiple of 6 plus 3) would be 15, 21, 27, etc.

( ) Repeat instruction in parentheses as many times as specified. For example: "(K 3, p 2) 5 times" means to do all that is specified in parentheses 5 times in all.

Place a marker in work Mark with a safety pin a certain point in the work, to use as a guide in taking future measurements.

Place a marker on needle Place a safety pin, paper clip, or bought plastic stitch marker on the needle, between stitches. It is slipped from one needle to the other to serve as a mark on following rows.

Slip a stitch When directions say "slip a stitch" or "sl 1," insert right needle in stitch to be slipped as if to purl and simply pass from left to right needle without working it.

TO BEGIN KNITTING: For a practice piece, use knitting worsted and No. 8 needles.

To cast on

Make a slip loop several inches from yarn end and insert point of needle through it (*see first diagram*). Tighten loop. Hold needle with tight-

ened loop in left hand. Hold second needle in right hand, with yarn in working position as shown in diagram below. Insert point of right

needle in loop on left needle from left to right. With index finger, bring the yarn over the

point of right needle as shown above. Draw the yarn through the loop, as below.

Insert left needle through new loop (*see below*) and remove right needle. You now have 2 stitches cast on. You can make the 3rd and all

succeeding stitches in the same way, or, for a stronger edge, you can insert right needle between stitches just below left needle instead of through loops (*see below*).

Cast on 15 stitches for a practice swatch. You are now ready to begin knitting.

KNIT STITCH

Hold needle with cast-on stitches in left hand. Insert right needle in front of first stitch on left needle from left to right. With right hand, bring yarn under and over the point of right needle and draw the yarn through the stitch, making loop on right needle; slip the old stitch off the left needle. This completes first stitch of row. Repeat in each stitch until all stitches

have been knitted off left needle. Always push work along left needle so that stitch to be worked is near tip. When row is completed, you should have 15 stitches on the right needle, just as you had on the left originally. Count stitches occasionally to make sure that you keep the same number. At the end of row, turn work so needle with stitches is in your left hand. Continue working rows in this manner until work is uniform and you feel familiar with the stitch. When you knit each stitch in each row in this way, it is called garter stitch.

To bind off

You are now ready to finish off your practice piece. This process is called binding off. Loosely knit 2 stitches. With point of left needle, pick up first stitch and slide it over second; slip it off needle. * Knit next stitch and slip preceding one over it. Repeat from * across.

When you come to your last stitch, cut yarn about 3″ from the needle. Bring loose end through last stitch and pull tightly. Darn in end with tapestry needle so that it will not show.

PURL STITCH

Cast on 15 stitches for practice swatch. Insert right needle in front of first stitch on left needle from right to left. With right hand, bring yarn over the point of right needle and draw yarn through the stitch; slip old stitch off left needle. This completes first purl stitch. Keeping yarn in front of work, repeat in each stitch across.

The wrong side of a purl stitch is a knit stitch. The purl stitch is rarely used alone, so to practice the stitch it is best to proceed with stockinette stitch.

STOCKINETTE STITCH

Cast on 15 stitches for practice swatch. Purl first row: Turn work. Knit next row, purl next row. Repeat these last 2 rows until your work is uniform and you feel familiar with the purl stitch. Bind off. If you bind off on a purl row, purl the stitches instead of knitting them.

Note: The bumpy surface of stockinette stitch is the purl side (as above): the smooth surface (this is usually the right side of work) is the knit side. You have now learned the two simple and basic stitches from which all knitting is derived.

Ribbing

Ribbing is a combination of purling and knitting in which you alternate a specified number of stitches of each. The most common form is knit 2, purl 2. It is always worked so stitches fall in columns. Because of its elasticity, it is generally used for waistbands and neckbands. It is easy to rib if you look at the stitches facing you and purl the purl stitches and knit the knit stitches.

How to increase

First work knit (or purl) stitch as usual into front of stitch, but leave stitch on left needle; then knit (or purl) in back of this same stitch.

How to decrease

There are two ways of decreasing, and directions always tell you which one to use. The first, and most often used, direction will say "dec 1" and will specify where to do it. To do this, simply knit or purl 2 stitches together working as if they were 1 stitch.

The second way is used only on knit rows. Directions will say "sl 1, k 1, psso." To do this, slip 1 stitch (simply pass the stitch from left needle to right, without working it), knit the next stitch, then pass the slipped stitch over the knitted stitch.

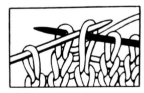

To make a yarn over

Yarn over automatically adds 1 stitch. It is used mostly in lace patterns, since it produces a hole in the work. To work it on a knit row, bring yarn under tip of right needle, up and over needle, then work next stitch.

199

On a purl row, bring yarn over right needle, around and to front again, then work next stitch (*see next diagram*).

A yarn over forms an extra loop on right needle. On next row, work it as you do other stitches.

How to attach new yarn

Plan to attach a new yarn at the beginning of a row. Tie in a single knot around old yarn, then knit several stitches with new yarn. Pull up old yarn so first stitch is same length as other stitches, and knot again. When work is completed, weave both ends into back.

Picking up dropped stitches

Beginners and even advanced knitters often drop a stitch or stitches. They must be picked up or they will "run" just like a stocking. Use a crochet hook. Catch the loose stitch and draw the horizontal thread of the row above

through it. Repeat until you reach the row on which you are working. Then place on needle. First diagram shows technique of picking up a knit stitch; the one below shows a purl stitch.

DUPLICATE STITCH

This is used to work a design on top of knitting. Thread a tapestry needle with contrasting color yarn and work as follows: draw yarn from wrong to right side through center of lower point of stitch. Insert needle at top right-hand side of same stitch. Then, holding needle in horizontal position, draw through to top left side of stitch. Insert again into base of same stitch. Keep work loose enough so it completely covers stitch being worked over. Almost any design that appears on a chart or graph can be worked in this stitch.

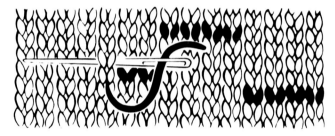

WORKING WITH TWO OR MORE COLORS

Fair Isle knitting

This term is used for a pattern where two colors are involved and the color changes every few stitches. The yarn not being used is carried on wrong side of work throughout the whole pattern.

To work it, yarn in the color used most is held in right hand as usual; the second color is held in the left hand. If yarn is carried more than 3 stitches, catch carried yarn in order to avoid having a long loop at back of work. Work as follows: * insert right needle in usual way, but before picking up yarn to work this stitch, slip right-hand needle under the carried yarn, work stitch in usual manner, slipping off carried yarn as stitch is completed. Work next stitch in usual way. Repeat from * across. Be careful not to draw yarn too tightly (work will pucker) or to work too loosely (loops will hang at back of work).

Double Knitting

Double knitting produces a double-layered stockinette stitch fabric with the smooth, knit side facing out on both sides, making the afghan both reversible and extra warm.

The colors used for one side will be reversed on the other side. For instance, if brown is the main color with details in white on one side, on the reverse side white will be the main color, with details in brown (see "New Bedford" afghan, page 72).

Several methods produce double knitting. The method given below was used by the knitter of the Reversible Tile afghan (page 21) and works very well for charted designs. Practice, using the small chart and directions below, until you feel comfortable with the technique before beginning your afghan.

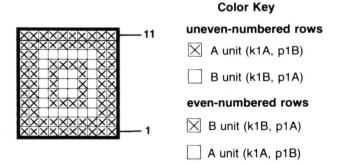

Color Key

uneven-numbered rows

☒ A unit (k1A, p1B)

☐ B unit (k1B, p1A)

even-numbered rows

☒ B unit (k1B, p1A)

☐ A unit (k1A, p1B)

To work your practice swatch, use size 10 (6.00 mm) knitting needles and two contrasting colors of knitting worsted (A and B). You may find it helpful to have someone read the directions aloud to you, step by step, so that you can knit without having to stop to look at the book.

With B cast on a st, then with A cast on the 2nd st; cast on the 3rd st with B, 4th st with A; continue in this manner, alternating colors A and B on each st, until all sts are cast on (20 for practice swatch).

For knitting, wind both strands of yarn around fingers of right hand as follows: wind yarn around little finger and under next (ring) finger, drop middle finger down to separate strands so that one strand lies under and one over middle finger, bring both strands up and over index finger. This makes it easier to control colors as needed without tangling them.

Note: On chart each square represents 1 unit, made up of 1 knit st for front layer and 1 purl st in other color for back layer.

Now follow chart and work as follows: **Row 1:** K 1 A, bring both strands of yarn to front of work (yf), p 1 B, bring both strands of yarn to back of work (yb)—one A unit completed; * k 1 A, yf, p 1 B, yb (another A unit); repeat from * across. Twist colors at end of rows to prevent holes in work. **Row 2:** * K 1 B, yf, p 1 B, yb (one B unit); repeat from * across. Note that on the work below the needle one layer is B and other layer is A. **Row 3:** Work 2 A units, 6 B units, 2 A units. **Row 4:** 2 B units, 1 A unit, 4 B units, 1 A unit, 2 B units. **Row 5:** 2 A units, 1 B unit, 1 A unit, 2 B units, 1 A unit, 1 B unit, 2 A units. **Row 6:** 2 B units, 1 A unit, 1 B unit, 2 A units, 1 B unit, 1 A unit, 2 B units. **Row 7:** Repeat Row 5. **Row 8:** Repeat Row 4. **Row 9:** Repeat Row 3. **Row 10:** Repeat Row 2. **Row 11:** Repeat Row 1. To bind off, k 1 B, yf, * p 1 A, yb, on right-hand needle sl B st over A st, k 1 B, yf, on right-hand needle sl A st over B st; repeat from * across until all sts are bound off.

Check to see that your swatch matches chart, and note how design reverses on other side. If you feel comfortable with the technique of double knitting, you are ready to start your afghan; otherwise, practice until you do feel comfortable.

As you work your afghan, mark off completed rows on chart and, if desired, use markers to section off areas to keep your place. If possible, work when you have quiet, uninterrupted time, because working complex patterns in double knit requires a great deal of concentration, especially if this is a new technique for you.

BLOCKING: To ensure a smooth, professional look, block pieces first, then sew together. If you have laundered your work, block it while still damp. If work has not been laundered, dampen by rolling up in large damp towel overnight. Place dampened work on a flat, padded surface. Gently shape it to desired measurements; pin to surface, using rust-proof pins, preferably ballpoint. Let dry thoroughly before unpinning. (*Note:* Do not use an iron for blocking, especially on synthetic yarns, which can melt.)

JOINING EDGES: Seams should be as invisible as possible. Thread a tapestry needle with same yarn as afghan. There are two methods of sewing. The first makes a neat, flat seam. Place two pieces to be joined side by side, flat on surface and with right sides up. Draw sewing yarn through first stitch at bottom edge of one piece, then draw through corresponding stitch of other piece. Continue in this manner, just picking up edge stitch of each piece, until seam is complete. The second method is used on shaped edges, as in sewing in a sleeve. With right sides facing, sew just inside edge, using a backstitch. Leave stitches loose enough to provide elasticity.

Embroidery Stitches

BACKSTITCH

Work from right to left. Bring needle up a short distance from start of line to be covered; insert it at start of line. Bring out an equal distance ahead along line; draw needle through.

CROSS-STITCH

Make a row of slanting stitches, working each stitch over a crocheted stitch of background. This forms a row of the first half of each cross. Work back over these stitches, completing the second half, as shown. You can work cross stitches individually and in any direction, but they must all be crossed in the same direction.

To work cross-stitch over afghan stitch or single crochet, see page 195.

FRENCH KNOT

Bring needle up at point where knot is to be made. Wind thread two or three times around point of needle; insert in fabric as close as possible to spot where thread emerged (but not in exact spot) and pull to wrong side, holding twists in place.

LAZY-DAISY STITCH

Bring thread up in center of "flower." Hold the thread down with thumb; insert needle close to or in exact spot where thread emerged and bring out desired distance below; draw through over working thread. Then tie down with a tiny stitch made over loop as shown. Make similar stitches to form a circle around same center point. Diagram shows them separated for clarity, but they can be made in same center hole.

SATIN STITCH

Bring needle up at one edge of area to be covered, insert needle at opposite edge, and return to starting line by carrying it underneath fabric. Make stitches close enough together to cover background fabric completely. Satin stitches should not be so long that they look loose and untidy. You can divide large areas to be covered into small sections.

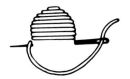

Index

For information on how you can have **Better Homes and Gardens** delivered to your door, write to: Mr. Robert Austin, P.O. Box 4536, Des Moines, IA 50336.